WORLD
LEADERS

People Who Shaped the World

WORLD LEADERS

People Who Shaped the World

North & South America

Rob Nagel • Anne Commire

AN IMPRINT OF
GALE RESEARCH INC.

World Leaders:
People Who Shaped the World

Rob Nagel and Anne Commire

Staff

Sonia Benson, U·X·L *Associate Developmental Editor*
Kathleen L. Witman, U·X·L *Assistant Developmental Editor*
Thomas L. Romig, U·X·L *Publisher*

Mary Kelley, *Production Associate*
Evi Seoud, *Assistant Production Manager*
Mary Beth Trimper, *Production Director*

Pamela A. E. Galbreath, *Cover and Page Designer*
Cynthia Baldwin, *Art Director*

Keith Reed, *Permissions Associate (Pictures)*
Margaret A. Chamberlain, *Permissions Supervisor (Pictures)*

The Graphix Group, *Typesetting*

Library of Congress Cataloging-in-Publication Data
World leaders: people who shaped the world / {edited by} Rob Nagel,
    Anne Commire.
        p. cm.
    Includes biographical references and index.
    ISBN 0-8103-9768-4 (set)
    1. Kings and rulers --Biography. 2. Heads of state--Biography. 3. Revolutionaries--
Biography. 4. Statesmen--Biography. I. Nagel, Rob. II. Commire, Anne.
D107.W65 1994
    920.02--dc20   94-20544
                                                                                       CIP
                                                                                        AC

This book is printed on acid-free paper that meets the minimum requirements of American National Standard for Information Sciences—Permanence Paper for Printed Library Materials, ANSI Z39.48-1984.

ISBN 0-8103-9768-4 (Set)

ISBN 0-8103-9769-2 (Volume 1)
ISBN 0-8103-9770-6 (Volume 2)
ISBN 0-8103-9771-4 (Volume 3)

Printed in the United States of America

Published simultaneously in the United Kingdom by Gale Research International Limited (An affiliated company of Gale Research Inc.)

Contents

VOLUME 3: NORTH AND SOUTH AMERICA

Preface

Through 120 biographical sketches in three volumes, *World Leaders: People Who Shaped the World* presents a diverse range of historical figures. Many of those profiled are political or military leaders whose achievements have been evident and far-reaching. Others featured may not be as conspicuous to the beginning student of history, but their achievements—considering the social context of the eras in which they lived and the barriers against which they fought—are no less great.

The individuals chosen for inclusion in *World Leaders* fall into one or more of the following categories:

- Those who significantly changed their nation or empire, affecting its—or the world's—course permanently or for a very long time.
- Those who exhibited great qualities in many areas—military, politics, art, religion, philosophy.
- Those who struggled against the forced limitations of gender, race, or social standing to achieve their ideals, leaving a trail for others to follow.

• Those who offered the world new ideas, options, or directions.

Each volume of *World Leaders* begins with a listing of the leaders by country and a timeline showing the chronological relationship among the profiled leaders, the incidents marking their lives, and certain other historical events.

Many sketches in *World Leaders* begin with a short discussion of the social or political environment in which these individuals arose. Where possible, childhood and educational experiences of the chosen leaders have been highlighted. Philosophical or religious ideas or movements that directed the course of the leaders' actions are explained in the text. Some of these ideas or movements, such as Stoicism or the Enlightenment, are given a fuller discussion in sidebars, more than a dozen of which are sprinkled throughout the three volumes. Other sidebars present varied topics—from the U.S. cost in the Vietnam War to a Shaker hymn—that are both informative and interesting.

Each biographical sketch in *World Leaders* contains a portrait of the profiled leader and the date and the place of that person's birth and death, or the dates of his or her reign. To provide readers with a clearer understanding of the geographical descriptions in the text, maps are placed within some sketches. A comprehensive subject index concludes each volume.

Acknowledgments

We wish to extend a humble note of thanks to the U·X·L family: Tom Romig, for graciously handing us this project; Kathleen Witman, for insightfully emending the style of the text; and, finally, Sonia Benson, for gently shepherding the work to its completion.

We welcome any comments on this work and suggestions for future volumes of *World Leaders*. Please write: Editors, *World Leaders,* U·X·L, Gale Research Inc., 835 Penobscot Bldg., Detroit, Michigan 48226-4094; call toll-free: 1-800-877-4253; or fax: 313-961-6348.

World Leaders by Country

A listing of leaders by the central country or countries in which they ruled or made changes. When possible, ancient empires, city-states, and kingdoms have been listed with an asterisk under the modern-day country in which they were once located.

Argentina:

José de San Martín
(1778-1850)
Eva Marie Duarte de Perón
(1919-1952)
Juan Domingo Perón
(1895-1974)

Assyria (ancient empire including vast region of western Asia):
Ashurbanipal
(c. 700-c. 626 B.C.)

Babylon (ancient city-state near present day Baghdad, Iraq):

Hammurabi
(ruled c. 1792-1759 B.C.)

Bolivia:

Simón Bolívar
(1783-1830)

Canada:

Samuel de Champlain
(c. 1570-1635)

Carthage (city-state in present-day Tunisia):
Hannibal
(247-183 B.C.)

China:

Chiang Kai-shek
  (1887-1975)
Confucius
  (c. 551-c. 479 B.C.)
Lao-tzu
  (c. sixth century B.C.)
Mao Zedong
  (1893-1976)
Qin Shi Huang-di
  (259-210 B.C.)
Zhao Kuang-yin
  (927-976)

Colombia:

Simón Bolívar
  (1783-1830)

Cuba:

Ernesto "Ché" Guevara
  (1928-1967)
José Martí
  (1853-1895)

Denmark:

Canute I, the Great
  (c. 995-1035)
Margaret I
  (1353-1412)

Egypt:

Cleopatra VII
  (69-30 B.C.)
Hatshepsut
  (c. 1520-c. 1468 B.C.)
Moses
  (c. late 13th century–
  c. early 11th century B.C.)

Gamal Abdal Nasser
  (1918-1970)
Ptolemy I Soter
  (367-285 B.C.)
Ramses II
  (c. 1315-c. 1225 B.C.)

England:

Alfred the Great
  (848-c. 900)
Canute I, the Great
  (c. 995-1035)
Winston Churchill
  (1874-1965)
Elizabeth I
  (1533-1603)
Victoria
  (1819-1901)
William the Conqueror
  (c. 1027-1087)

Ethiopia:

Haile Selassie I
  (1892-1975)

France:

Eleanor of Aquitaine
  (1122-1204)
Joan of Arc
  (c. 1412-1431)
Louis XIV
  (1638-1715)
Napoleon I Bonaparte
  (1769-1821)

Germany:

Adolf Hitler
  (1889-1945)

Martin Luther
   (1483-1546)
Rudolf I, of Habsburg
   (1218-1291)

Haiti:

Toussaint L'Ouverture
   (1743-1803)

Hungary:

Stephen I
   (c. 973-1038)

India:

Akbar
   (1542-1605)
Mohandas Gandhi
   (1869-1948)
Jawaharlal Nehru
   (1889-1964)
Siddhartha
   (c. 563-c. 483 B.C.)
Mother Teresa
   (1910—)

Iran (formerly Persia):

Abbas I
   (1571-1629)
Cyrus II, the Great
   (c. 590-c. 529)
Ruhollah Khomeini
   (c. 1902-1989)
Zoroaster
   (c. 588-c. 511 B.C.)

Ireland:

Saint Patrick
   (c. 395-c. 460)

Israel:

David Ben-Gurion
   (1886-1973)
King David
   (ruled 1010-970 B.C.)
Jesus of Nazareth
   (c. 6 B.C.-c. A.D. 26)
Moses
   (c. late 13th century–
   c. early 11th century B.C.)

Italy (also see Roman Empire):

Francis of Assisi
   (1182-1226)
John XXIII
   (1881-1963)

Japan:

Fujiwara Michinaga
   (966-1028)

Kenya:

Jomo Kenyatta
   (1891-1978)

Macedonia:

Alexander the Great
   (356-323 B.C.)

Mexico:

Juana Inés de la Cruz
   (1648-1695)
Emiliano Zapata
   (1879-1919)
Tenochtitlán:

Moctezuma II
(c. 1480-1520)

Mongolia:

Genghis Khan
(c. 1162-1227)

Norway:

Canute I, the Great
(c. 995-1035)
Margaret I
(1353-1412)

North Vietnam:

Ho Chi Minh
(1890-1969)

Pannonia] (area in present-
day Hungary and eastern
Austria):

Attila the Hun
(c. 370-453)

Prussia (former state of
Central Europe, including
parts of present-day
Germany and Poland):

Frederick II, the Great
(1712-1786)
Karl Marx
(1818-1883)

Roman Empire:

Augustus
(63 B.C.-A.D. 14)
Julius Caesar

(100-44 B.C.)
Charlemagne
(c. 742-814)
Charles V
(1500-1558)
Constantine I
(285-337)
Frederick I (Barbarossa)
(1123-1190)
Gregory I, the Great
(c. 540-604)
Marcus Aurelius
(121-180)
Otto I, the Great
(912-973)
Rudolf I, of Habsburg
(1218-1291)

Russia:

Catherine II, the Great
(1729-1796)
Gorbachev, Mikhail
(1931—)
Ivan IV, the Terrible
(1530-1584)
Vladimir Lenin
(1870-1924)
Alexander Nevsky
(c. 1220-1263)

Saudi Arabia:

Muhammad (c. 570-632)

Scotland:

Mary, Queen of Scots
(1542-1587)
Robert I, the Bruce
(1274-1329)

Senegal:

Léopold Sédar Senghor
   (1906—)

Spain:

Ferdinand II
   (1452-1516)
Isabella I
   (1451-1504)

Sweden:

Gustavus Adolphus
   (1594-1632)
Margaret I
   (1353-1412)

Syria:

Palmyra:
Zenobia
   (ruled 267-272)

Turkey:

Byzantine Empire:
Irene of Athens
   (c. 752-803)
Theodora
   (c. 500-548)
Ottoman Empire:
Osman I
   (1259-1326)
Suleiman
   (c. 1494-1566)

United Republic of Tanzania:

Julius K. Nyerere
   (1922—)

United States:

Jane Addams
   (1860-1935)
Susan B. Anthony
   (1820-1906)
William Bradford
   (1590-1657)
Chief Joseph
   (1840-1905)
Crazy Horse
   (1841-1877)
Frederick Douglass
   (1818-1895)
W. E. B. Du Bois
   (1868-1963)
Benjamin Franklin
   (1706-1790)
Ulysses S. Grant
   (1822-1885)
Thomas Jefferson
   (1743-1826)
John F. Kennedy
   (1917-1963)
Martin Luther King, Jr.
   (1929-1968)
Mother Ann Lee
   (1736-1784)
Robert E. Lee
   (1807-1870)
Abraham Lincoln
   (1809-1865)
Malcolm X
   (1925-1965)
Thurgood Marshall
   (1908-1993)
Increase Mather
   (1639-1723)
Thomas Paine
   (1737-1809)

Eleanor Roosevelt
(1884-1962)
Franklin Roosevelt
(1882-1945)
Sitting Bull
(c. 1830-1890)
John Smith
(c. 1580-1631)
Elizabeth Cady Stanton
(1815-1902)
Tecumseh
(c. 1768-1813)
Sojourner Truth
(c. 1797-1883)
Harriet Tubman
(c. 1820-1913)
Booker T. Washington
(1856-1915)
George Washington
(1732-1799)
Roger Williams
(c. 1603-1683)

Venezuela:

Simón Bolívar
(1783-1830)

WORLD
LEADERS

People Who Shaped the World

Egyptian Pyramids

Timeline

3000 B.C.   **1500 B.C.**   **550 B.C.**

1010-970 B.C.

1: David unites
Israel and Judah
in a kingdom
centered at
Jerusalem

c. 1792-1750 B.C.

1: Hammurabi creates empire of Babylonia
and devises his famous law code

---

c. 2680–1200 B.C. • Ancient Egypt

c. 2680-2526 B.C. • 1: Building of the Great Pyramids near Giza,
Egypt

c. 1490-1470 B.C. • 1: Hatshepsut proclaims herself "king" of
Egypt and rules as pharaoh

c. 1250 B.C. • 1: Ramses II builds colossal temple at Abu Simbel

c. 1200 B.C. • 1: Moses leads the Hebrews out of slavery in Egypt
to the land of Canaan

---

c. 670-626 B.C.

1: Ashurbanipal
creates a great
library in
Nineveh, the
capital city of the
Assyrian Empire

---

c. 6th century B.C. • Philosophy and Religion

c. 6th century B.C. • 1: Lao-tzu reportedly writes his moral
philosophy in the *Tao Te Ching*

c. 550-511 B.C. • 1: Zoroaster spreads his new religion
throughout the Persian Empire

c. 528 B.C. • 1: Siddhartha founds new religion of Buddhism in
India

c. 520 B.C. • 1: Confucius begins teaching a new moral
philosophy in China

---

c. 550 B.C.

1: Cyrus II, the Great
conquers Media and begins
building the Persian Empire

1 = Volume 1: Asia and Africa
2 = Volume 2: Europe
3 = Volume 3: North and South America

550 B.C.   **200B.C.**   **0**

221 B.C.

1: Qin Shi Huang-di unifies China

c. 6 B.C.

1: Jesus of Nazareth born

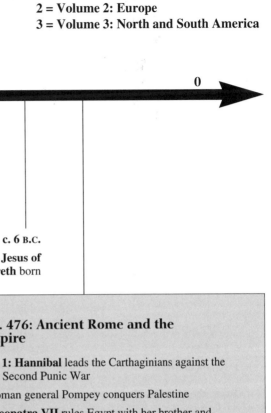

218 B.C.–A.D. 476: Ancient Rome and the Roman Empire

218-201 B.C. • 1: Hannibal leads the Carthaginians against the Romans in the Second Punic War

63 B.C. • 1: Roman general Pompey conquers Palestine

51 B.C. • 1: Cleopatra VII rules Egypt with her brother and husband, Ptolemy XII

44 B.C. • 2: Julius Caesar becomes Roman dictator for life and is then assassinated

27 B.C. • 2: Augustus becomes "President of the Republic" of Rome

c. A.D. 170 • 2: Marcus Aurelius begins writing his *Meditations* while leading battles for the Roman Empire

267-272 • 1: Zenobia, the "warrior queen" of Palmyra, challenges the Roman Empire

330 • 2: Constantine I founds the Byzantine Empire at Constantinople

451 • 2: Attila leads the Huns against the Romans

476 • 1, 2: West Roman Empire falls

323 B.C.

1: Ptolemy I Soter founds the Ptolemaic dynasty that rules Egypt for nearly 300 years

332 B.C.

2: Alexander the Great conquers Egypt and founds the city of Alexandria

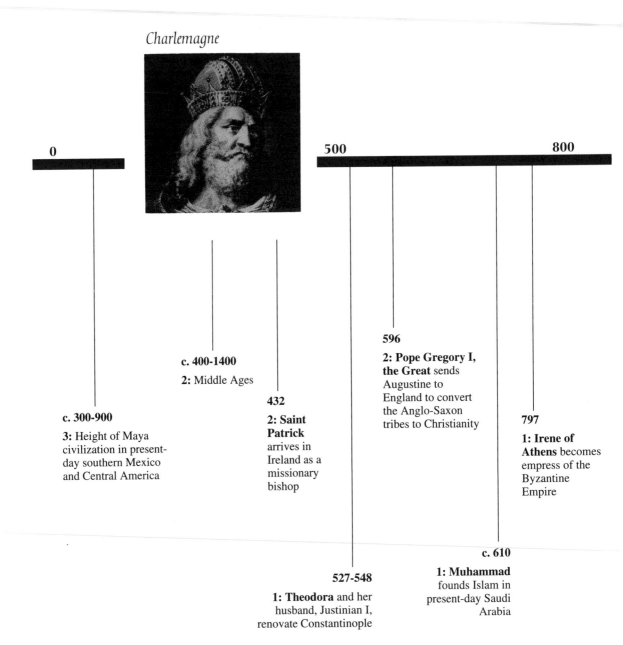

Charlemagne

0

500

800

c. 400-1400
2: Middle Ages

432
2: Saint Patrick arrives in Ireland as a missionary bishop

596
2: Pope Gregory I, the Great sends Augustine to England to convert the Anglo-Saxon tribes to Christianity

797
1: Irene of Athens becomes empress of the Byzantine Empire

c. 300-900
3: Height of Maya civilization in present-day southern Mexico and Central America

527-548
1: Theodora and her husband, Justinian I, renovate Constantinople

c. 610
1: Muhammad founds Islam in present-day Saudi Arabia

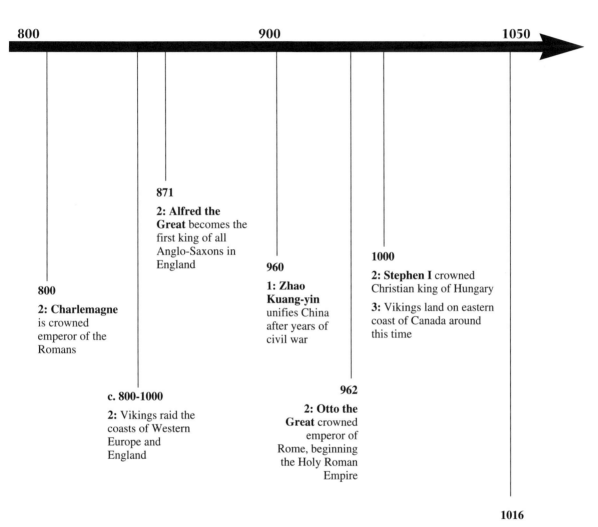

1 = Volume 1: Asia and Africa
2 = Volume 2: Europe
3 = Volume 3: North and South America

800   900   1050

871

2: Alfred the Great becomes the first king of all Anglo-Saxons in England

960

1: Zhao Kuang-yin unifies China after years of civil war

1000

2: Stephen I crowned Christian king of Hungary

3: Vikings land on eastern coast of Canada around this time

800

2: Charlemagne is crowned emperor of the Romans

c. 800-1000

2: Vikings raid the coasts of Western Europe and England

962

2: Otto the Great crowned emperor of Rome, beginning the Holy Roman Empire

1016

1: Fujiwara Michinaga assumes behind-the-scenes political power in Japan

2: Viking **Canute I, the Great** begins rule as king of England, Denmark, and Norway

Osman I

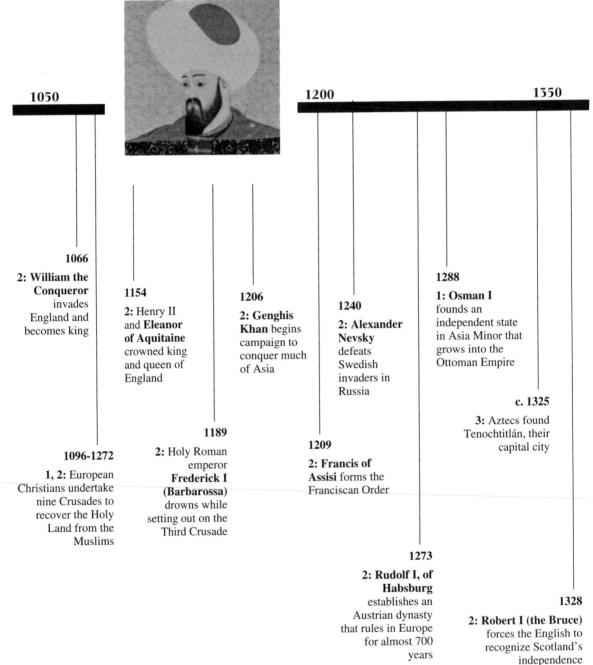

1050

1200

1350

1066

2: William the Conqueror invades England and becomes king

1154

2: Henry II and **Eleanor of Aquitaine** crowned king and queen of England

1206

2: Genghis Khan begins campaign to conquer much of Asia

1240

2: Alexander Nevsky defeats Swedish invaders in Russia

1288

1: Osman I founds an independent state in Asia Minor that grows into the Ottoman Empire

c. 1325

3: Aztecs found Tenochtitlán, their capital city

1096-1272

1, 2: European Christians undertake nine Crusades to recover the Holy Land from the Muslims

1189

2: Holy Roman emperor **Frederick I (Barbarossa)** drowns while setting out on the Third Crusade

1209

2: Francis of Assisi forms the Franciscan Order

1273

2: Rudolf I, of Habsburg establishes an Austrian dynasty that rules in Europe for almost 700 years

1328

2: Robert I (the Bruce) forces the English to recognize Scotland's independence

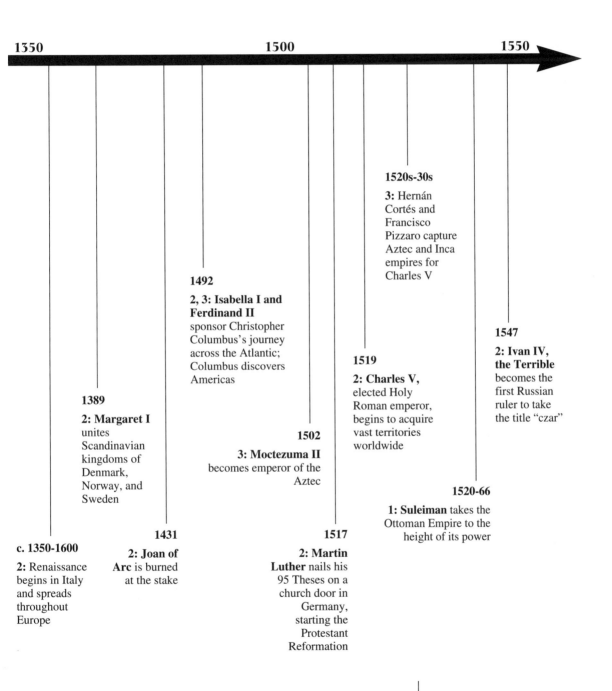

1 = **Volume 1: Asia and Africa**
2 = **Volume 2: Europe**
3 = **Volume 3: North and South America**

1350   1500   1550

1520s-30s

3: Hernán Cortés and Francisco Pizzaro capture Aztec and Inca empires for Charles V

1492

2, 3: Isabella I and Ferdinand II sponsor Christopher Columbus's journey across the Atlantic; Columbus discovers Americas

1547

2: Ivan IV, the Terrible becomes the first Russian ruler to take the title "czar"

1389

2: Margaret I unites Scandinavian kingdoms of Denmark, Norway, and Sweden

1519

2: Charles V, elected Holy Roman emperor, begins to acquire vast territories worldwide

1502

3: Moctezuma II becomes emperor of the Aztec

1520-66

1: Suleiman takes the Ottoman Empire to the height of its power

c. 1350-1600

2: Renaissance begins in Italy and spreads throughout Europe

1431

2: Joan of Arc is burned at the stake

1517

2: Martin Luther nails his 95 Theses on a church door in Germany, starting the Protestant Reformation

Elizabeth I

1550   **1600**   **1700**

1588

2: Elizabeth I's navy defeats the Spanish Armada

1611-30

2: Gustavus Adolphus forms a Swedish empire

1688

3: Increase Mather secures charter for the Massachusetts Bay Colony

1587

1: Abbas I begins rule as shah of Persia (Iran)

2: Mary, Queen of Scots is beheaded by the order of the English queen **Elizabeth I**

1654

2: Louis XIV is crowned king of France

1556

1: Akbar assumes throne of the Mughal Empire in India

1607–1636 • Settlements in North America

1607 • **3: John Smith** and others found Jamestown

1608 • **3: Samuel de Champlain** founds Quebec

1620 • **3: William Bradford** and other Puritans found Plymouth

1636 • **3: Roger Williams** founds Providence, Rhode Island

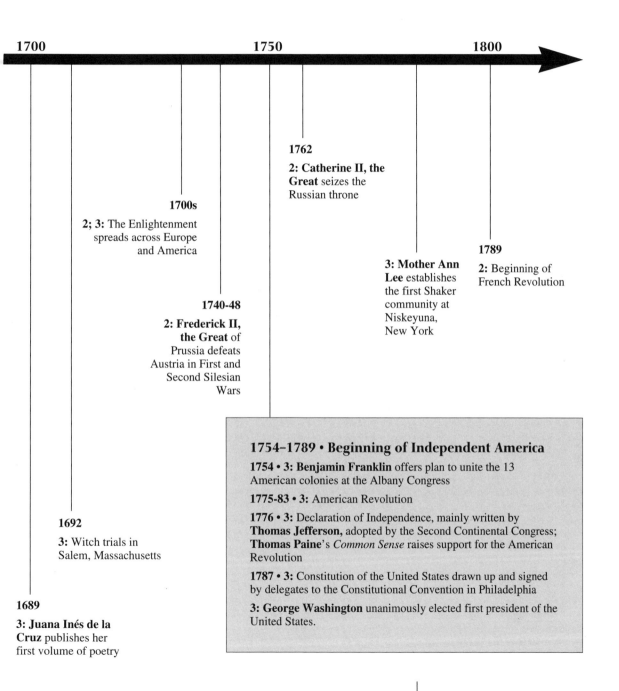

1 = Volume 1: Asia and Africa
2 = Volume 2: Europe
3 = Volume 3: North and South America

1700   1750   1800

1762

2: Catherine II, the Great seizes the Russian throne

1700s

2; 3: The Enlightenment spreads across Europe and America

1789

2: Beginning of French Revolution

3: Mother Ann Lee establishes the first Shaker community at Niskeyuna, New York

1740-48

2: Frederick II, the Great of Prussia defeats Austria in First and Second Silesian Wars

1754–1789 • Beginning of Independent America

1754 • 3: Benjamin Franklin offers plan to unite the 13 American colonies at the Albany Congress

1775-83 • 3: American Revolution

1776 • 3: Declaration of Independence, mainly written by **Thomas Jefferson,** adopted by the Second Continental Congress; **Thomas Paine**'s *Common Sense* raises support for the American Revolution

1787 • 3: Constitution of the United States drawn up and signed by delegates to the Constitutional Convention in Philadelphia

3: George Washington unanimously elected first president of the United States.

1692

3: Witch trials in Salem, Massachusetts

1689

3: Juana Inés de la Cruz publishes her first volume of poetry

Simón Bolívar

1800

1820

1850

1817

3: José de San Martín battles
Spanish forces in Chile

1837-1901

2: Reign of England's
Queen Victoria II

1812

3: Tecumseh and
English forces
capture Detroit

1819

3: Simón Bolívar
proclaimed president
of Greater Colombia

1848

3: Karl Marx and Friedrich Engels
publish the *Communist Manifesto*

1804

**2: Napoleon I
Bonaparte** is
crowned emperor
of France

1831–1870 • Slavery and the American Civil War

1831 • 3: Nat Turner leads a bloody slave uprising in Virginia

1841 • 3: Frederick Douglass gives his first abolitionist speech

1850 • 3: Harriet Tubman leads her first party of slaves to
freedom on the Underground Railroad; **Sojourner Truth**
publishes her autobiography, *Narrative of Sojourner Truth*

1859 • 3: Abolitionist John Brown is hanged after seizing the
government arsenal at Harpers Ferry, Virginia

1861-65 • 3: American Civil War

1862 • 3: Robert E. Lee defeats the Union forces at the Seven
Days' battle and the second battle of Bull Run

1863 • 3: Abraham Lincoln issues the Emancipation
Proclamation; **Ulysses S. Grant** defeats the Confederate forces at
Vicksburg

1865 • 3: Lee surrenders to Grant at Appomattox Courthouse;
Lincoln assassinated by John Wilkes Booth at Ford's Theater

1868 • 3: U.S. Congress adopts the Fourteenth Amendment,
recognizing former slaves as U.S. citizens

1870 • 3: Fifteenth Amendment of U.S. Constitution extends
voting rights to all black males

1812-15

2, 3: War of 1812
between the U.S.
and England

1801

**3: Toussaint
L'Ouverture**
conquers Spanish
colony of Santo
Domingo

Timeline

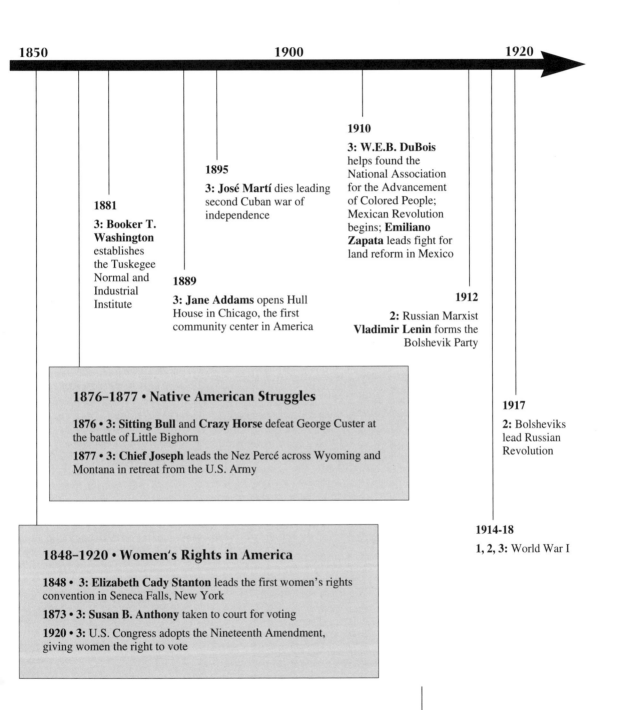

1 = **Volume 1: Asia and Africa**
2 = **Volume 2: Europe**
3 = **Volume 3: North and South America**

1850   1900   1920

1910

3: W.E.B. DuBois helps found the National Association for the Advancement of Colored People; Mexican Revolution begins; **Emiliano Zapata** leads fight for land reform in Mexico

1895

3: José Martí dies leading second Cuban war of independence

1881

3: Booker T. Washington establishes the Tuskegee Normal and Industrial Institute

1889

3: Jane Addams opens Hull House in Chicago, the first community center in America

1912

2: Russian Marxist **Vladimir Lenin** forms the Bolshevik Party

1876–1877 • Native American Struggles

1876 • 3: Sitting Bull and **Crazy Horse** defeat George Custer at the battle of Little Bighorn

1877 • 3: Chief Joseph leads the Nez Percé across Wyoming and Montana in retreat from the U.S. Army

1917

2: Bolsheviks lead Russian Revolution

1914-18

1, 2, 3: World War I

1848–1920 • Women's Rights in America

1848 • 3: Elizabeth Cady Stanton leads the first women's rights convention in Seneca Falls, New York

1873 • 3: Susan B. Anthony taken to court for voting

1920 • 3: U.S. Congress adopts the Nineteenth Amendment, giving women the right to vote

Adolf Hitler

1920

1935

1946

1940

2: Winston Churchill is named prime minister of England

1926

1: Chiang Kai-shek leads his Nationalist army in the Northern Expedition to unify China

1933

2: Adolf Hitler is named chancellor of Germany

3: Franklin D. Roosevelt begins his New Deal program

1939-45

1, 2, 3: World War II

1946

3: Eleanor Roosevelt appointed chairperson of the United Nations Commission on Human Rights

1935

1: Haile Selassie I leads his Ethiopian army against the invading Italian forces of Benito Mussolini

1929

3: Stock-market crash in the U.S. marks the beginning of the Great Depression

1946

3: Juan Domingo Perón elected president of Argentina

1919–1947 • Indian Independence

1919 • 1: Mohandas Gandhi organizes his first nationwide nonviolent demonstration protesting English rule in India

1947 • 1: Jawaharlal Nehru becomes the first prime minister of an independent India

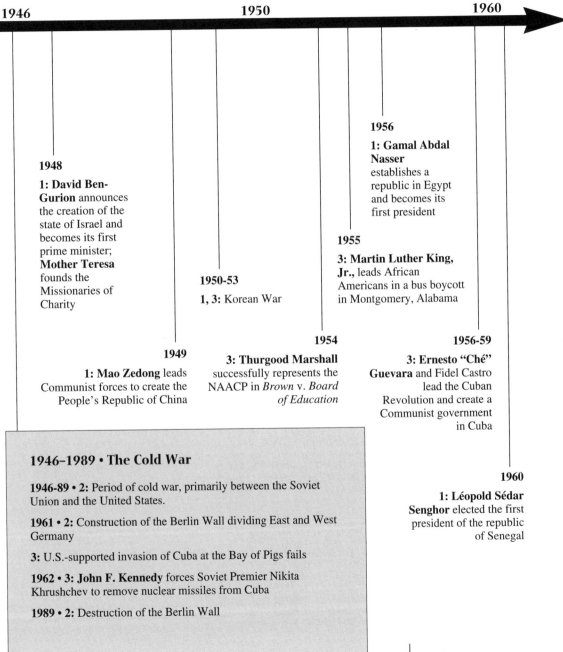

1 = Volume 1: Asia and Africa
2 = Volume 2: Europe
3 = Volume 3: North and South America

1946   1950   1960

1956

1: Gamal Abdal Nasser establishes a republic in Egypt and becomes its first president

1948

1: David Ben-Gurion announces the creation of the state of Israel and becomes its first prime minister; **Mother Teresa** founds the Missionaries of Charity

1955

3: Martin Luther King, Jr., leads African Americans in a bus boycott in Montgomery, Alabama

1950-53

1, 3: Korean War

1949

1: Mao Zedong leads Communist forces to create the People's Republic of China

1954

3: Thurgood Marshall successfully represents the NAACP in *Brown* v. *Board of Education*

1956-59

3: Ernesto "Ché" Guevara and Fidel Castro lead the Cuban Revolution and create a Communist government in Cuba

1960

1: Léopold Sédar Senghor elected the first president of the republic of Senegal

1946–1989 • The Cold War

1946-89 • 2: Period of cold war, primarily between the Soviet Union and the United States.

1961 • 2: Construction of the Berlin Wall dividing East and West Germany

3: U.S.-supported invasion of Cuba at the Bay of Pigs fails

1962 • 3: John F. Kennedy forces Soviet Premier Nikita Khrushchev to remove nuclear missiles from Cuba

1989 • 2: Destruction of the Berlin Wall

John F. Kennedy

1960

1965

1980

1962

**2: Pope John
XXI** opens the
Second Vatican
Council in Rome

1964

1: Jomo Kenyatta
becomes the first
president of the newly
independent Kenya;
Julius K. Nyerere
unites Tanganyika and
Zanzibar to form
Tanzania, and becomes
its first president

1969

3: U.S. astronaut
Neil Armstrong
becomes the first
person to walk
on the moon

1979

**1: Ruhollah
Khomeini**
creates an
Islamic state
in Iran

1963–1968 • Assassinations in America

1963 • 3: John F. Kennedy assassinated in Dallas, Texas

1965 • 3: Malcolm X assassinated in New York

1968 • 3: Martin Luther King, Jr., assassinated in Memphis,
Tennessee

1954–1975 • Conflict in Vietnam

1954 • 1: Ho Chi Minh becomes president of Communist North
Vietnam after Vietnamese forces defeat the French

1961-73 • 3: U.S. takes part in the Vietnam War

1975 • 1: North Vietnam defeats South Vietnam, uniting the
country under a Communist government

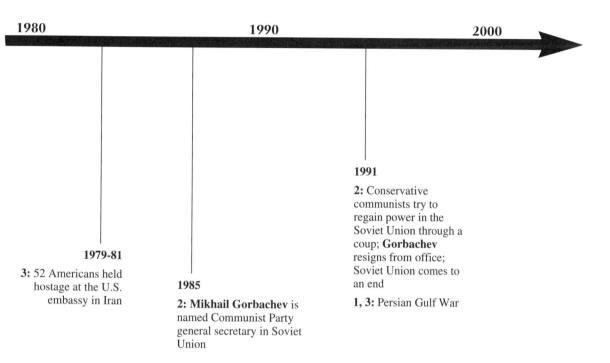

1 = Volume 1: Asia and Africa
2 = Volume 2: Europe
3 = Volume 3: North and South America

1980   1990   2000

1991

2: Conservative communists try to regain power in the Soviet Union through a coup; **Gorbachev** resigns from office; Soviet Union comes to an end

1, 3: Persian Gulf War

1979-81

3: 52 Americans held hostage at the U.S. embassy in Iran

1985

2: Mikhail Gorbachev is named Communist Party general secretary in Soviet Union

Mikhail Gorbachev

Timeline

Jane Addams

American social reformer

Born September 6, 1860,
Cedarville, Illinois

Died May 21, 1935,
Chicago, Illinois

The Industrial Revolution took place in America in the years immediately following the Civil War. The boom of machines and manufacturing required a cheap and plentiful labor force around the same time millions of Europeans swarmed into American cities. By 1890, 80 percent of the people living in Chicago were immigrants or children of immigrants. Most cities, however, did not have the resources to handle such a rapid growth of people. Many immigrants were forced to settle in slums, living lives of poverty and hopelessness. Problems were only worsened by the fact that several different ethnic groups were huddled into one area.

Jane Addams was one of the first people in America who sought to improve the lives of these desperate poor. In Chicago she founded a settlement house (community center) called Hull House. Her work toward social improvements in Chicago soon brought about changes throughout the country. Later in her life, Addams focused her energies on international problems, becoming a dedicated leader in the peace movement.

"Jane Addams was one of the first people in America who sought to improve the lives of these desperate poor."

Addams was born in Cedarville, Illinois, only seven months before the start of the Civil War. Her mother died when she was two years old, and Addams was raised by her father, John Huy Addams. A successful businessman and politician, John Addams helped build Cedarville into a thriving community. He passed on to his daughter his belief in the ideals of hard work, achievement, democracy, and equality. He also imparted to Jane a high moral sense of responsibility and purpose, traits of his Quaker faith.

Jane Addams was torn because of these teachings. She had learned that it was essential to do something important with her life, yet she grew up in a society that gave women the single role of homemaker. Even though her father encouraged her education, he believed its purpose was to make her a better wife and mother. Addams, however, desired more and enrolled in nearby Rockford College beginning in 1877. Upon her graduation in 1881, she planned to attend Women's Medical College in Philadelphia and, later, to work as a doctor among the poor.

European Trip Gives Her Insight

These plans went awry when a mysterious illness struck Addams. An unknown back ailment forced her to drop out of Women's Medical College at the end of her first year. She underwent an operation and was confined to bed for six months. After recovering her health, she went to Europe to figure out what to do with her life. In her travels through European cities, Addams was deeply moved after seeing the dismal conditions in which the poor lived. Her visit to Toynbee Hall in England opened her eyes to what could be done to help these people. Founded by Samuel Barnett in 1884, Toynbee Hall was the very first community center established to tackle the problems of poverty in the cities.

Addams returned to America determined to achieve similar improvements. On September 8, 1889, she opened Hull House on Halsted Street in the middle of Chicago's worst immigrant slum. By living at the center, Addams and her fellow reformers believed they could better understand the problems of the poor. Hull House offered the people of the surrounding neighborhood hot lunches, child care services, tutoring in English, and parties. Addams tried to develop the idea of a neighborhood spirit. She encouraged the immigrants to work together to do what they could to improve the conditions of their neighborhood. Addams also petitioned the city government to pave better streets and to build public baths, parks, and playgrounds.

Seeks Reform on a National Stage

Local activities to improve social conditions soon spread to state and national levels. Community centers sprang up across America. Hull House became a meeting place for intellectuals and reformers like the physician Alice Hamilton and the philosopher and educator John Dewey. Investigations into every social problem took place at Hull House. National campaigns were developed for issues such as women's suffrage (the right to vote) and labor rights of women and children. Addams gave lectures and wrote articles and books detailing the work performed at the center. Her book *Twenty Years at Hull-House,* published in 1910, did much to promote her work. In 1911 the National Federation of Settlements and Neighborhood Centers was established with Addams serving as its first president.

Addams spent her life working to overcome social inequalities. When World War I began in 1914, she became an outspoken member of the pacifist (peace) movement. The following year she joined other peace-minded women in forming the Women's Peace Party. The party sought a peaceful end to the war and worked to establish a permanent international peacekeeping organization. National pride was high both during and after the war, and pacifists were criticized for their activities. Remaining firm in her beliefs, Addams helped organize the Women's International League for Peace and Freedom. She served as its president until her death. For her dedicated work toward peace, Addams was awarded (along with fellow activist Nicholas Murray Butler) the Noble Peace Prize in 1931. Four year later, she died of cancer in Chicago.

Susan B. Anthony

Leader in Woman Suffrage Movement

Born February 5, 1820,
Adams, Massachusetts

Died March 13, 1906,
Rochester, New York

"Through Anthony's determined work, many professional fields became open to women by the end of the nineteenth century."

Susan B. Anthony's Quaker upbringing greatly influenced the role she played in nineteenth-century America. Quakers, properly known as the Religious Society of Friends, arose as a religious group in the mid-seventeenth century in England. They founded their religion on the belief that priests and places of organized worship are not necessary for a person to experience God. They feel there is an "inner light" inside everyone that can guide them to divine truth. Quakers do not believe in armed conflict or slavery, and they were among the first groups to practice full equality between men and women. Other American women did not experience the freedom and respect Anthony did while growing up. She worked to change that disparity, by becoming a leader in the crusade for women's rights.

Born in 1820 in a New England farmhouse, Anthony was the daughter of Lucy Read Anthony and Daniel Anthony, a cotton-mill owner. Her father instilled in his children the ideas of self-reliance, self-discipline, and self-worth. Since Quakers stressed a moral life, both her parents were strong supporters of the abolitionist (antislavery) and the temperance (avoidance of alcohol) movements. They also believed in the importance of work, and Anthony performed many tasks in her father's factory while attending school.

After having completed her schooling at the age of 17, Anthony began teaching in schools in rural New York state. Because it was regarded as similar to motherhood, teaching was one of the few professions open to women at the time. It allowed them to establish their own identities by gaining economic independence. However, teaching wages for men and women differed greatly. Anthony's weekly salary was equal to one-fifth of that received by her male colleagues. When she protested this inequality, she lost her job. She then secured a better position as principal of the Girls' Department of the Canajoharie Academy in Rochester, New York.

From Temperance to Women's Rights

In 1849, after having taught for over ten years, Anthony found her spirit drained and her professional future bleak. She focused her energies on social improvements and joined the local temperance society, only to be faced with inequality once again. After she was denied the chance to speak at a Sons of Temperance meeting because she was a woman, she founded the Daughters of Temperance, the first women's temperance organization. She began writing temperance articles for the *Lily,* the first woman-owned newspaper in the United States. Through the paper's editor, Amelia Bloomer, Anthony met women involved in the abolitionist movement and in the recently formed woman suffrage (right to vote) movement.

At a temperance meeting in 1851, Anthony met women's rights leader Elizabeth Cady Stanton (see **Elizabeth Cady Stanton**). They formed a deep personal friendship and a political bond that would last for the rest of their lives. From this point on, Anthony worked tirelessly for the woman suffrage movement. She lectured on women's rights and organized a series of state and national conventions on the issue. She collected signatures for a petition to grant women the right to vote and to own property. Her hard work helped. In 1860 the New York state legislature passed the Married Women's Property Act. It allowed women to enter into contracts and to control their own earnings and property.

During the Civil War, Anthony and most other members of the women's movement worked toward the emancipation of the slaves. In 1863 she helped form the Women's Loyal League, which supported U.S. President Abraham Lincoln's policies. After the war, Anthony and others tried to link women's suffrage with that of the freed slaves. They were unsuccessful. The Fifteenth Amendment, finally adopted in 1870, extended voting rights only to black men. Now without abolitionist support, Anthony and Stanton formed their own organization, the National Woman Suffrage Association.

Brought to Trial for Voting

The Fourteenth Amendment, adopted in 1868, had declared that all people born in the United States were citizens and that no legal privileges could be denied to any citizen. Anthony decided to challenge this amendment. Saying that women were citizens and the amendment did not restrict the privilege of voting to men, she registered to vote in Rochester, New York, on November 1, 1872. Four days later, she and fifteen other women voted in the presidential election. All sixteen women were arrested three weeks later, but only Anthony was brought before a court. Her trial, *United States v. Susan B. Anthony,* began on June 17, 1873. The presiding judge opposed women's suffrage and wrote his decision before the trial even had started. Refusing to let Anthony testify, he ordered the jury to find her guilty, then sentenced her to pay a $100 fine. She refused, and no further action was taken against her.

Anthony continued to campaign for women's rights after this. Between 1881 and 1886, she and Stanton published three volumes of the *History of Woman Suffrage,* a collection of writings about the movement's struggle. In 1890 they strengthened the suffrage cause by forming the larger National American Woman Suffrage Association. Through Anthony's determined work, many professional fields became open to women by the end of the nineteenth century. At the time of her death in 1906, however, only four states—Wyoming, Colorado, Idaho, and Utah—had granted suffrage to women. But her crusade carried on, and in 1920 Congress adopted the Nineteenth Amendment, finally giving women throughout America the right to vote.

Simón Bolívar

South American revolutionary leader

Born July 24, 1783,
Caracas, Venezuela

Died December 17, 1830,
near Santa Marta, Colombia

"Although Bolívar's dream of a long-lasting Greater Colombia faded, his successes helped create independent countries in South America, one of which bears his name today."

Beginning in the sixteenth century, Spain conquered lands and people in Central and South America for the glory of gold and God. For almost the next three hundred years, Spain brutally controlled its colonies of New Spain (present-day Mexico) and New Granada (present-day Venezuela, Colombia, Panama, and Ecuador). In the early 1800s, when the corrupt government in Spain fell to the French emperor Napoleon (see **Napoleon I Bonaparte**), the colonists seized their chance for independence. Out of this South American revolution rose a leader, Simón Bolívar, who led his people against the Spanish for over ten years. By 1819 he created the independent Greater Colombia out of much of the former New Granada and was declared its first president. Although Bolívar's dream of a long-lasting Greater Colombia faded, his successes helped create independent countries in South America, one of which bears his name today.

Bolívar's education prepared him well for the revolution. He was born in 1783 in Caracas, Venezuela, to Don Juan Vincente, a landowning aristocrat, and Doña Maria de la Concepcion Palacios y Blanco. By the time he was nine, both of his parents had died. His uncle, Esteban Palacios, then became his guardian and placed his education in the hands of a tutor, Simón Rodríguez. He introduced the young Bolívar to the ideas of the Enlightenment, a philosophic movement of that time that stressed man's reason as a guide to life. Bolívar was deeply affected by the political writings of the Frenchman Charles de Montesquieu and the Swiss Jean Jacques Rousseau. Simply put, they believed that governments should guarantee the rights of everyone and that governments, when ruled by the majority, will seek out the common good in society.

Travels in Europe Broaden Education

When he was 16, Bolívar went to Spain to travel and to complete his education. In 1802, while in Madrid, Spain, he married María Teresa Rodríguez del Toro, the daughter of a Spanish nobleman. They returned to Caracas, but within a year she died of yellow fever. Heartbroken, Bolívar went back to Europe, traveling throughout the continent. He learned to speak French, Italian, German, and English in addition to his native Spanish. He increased his studies of Enlightenment philosophy and filled his mind with the ideas of freedom, liberty, and human rights. Upon returning to Venezuela in 1807, Bolívar freed all the slaves working on his estate.

South American independence began in Caracas in April 1810 when the colonial governor was removed and a new junta (governing body) was established. The junta sent Bolívar on a mission to England to purchase arms and to secure help for the movement. Shortly after he returned with a cargo of arms in 1811, Venezuela formally declared its independence. Spanish forces rallied to capture the colony, and the patriot forces, led by General Francisco de Miranda, soon fell. Bolívar fled to present-day Colombia to gain support for a new invasion of Caracas.

Under the Spanish, Venezuelan cities were plundered, women were brutalized, and prisoners were mercilessly killed. In May 1813 Bolívar began his march through Venezuela. In just 90 days, he and his army destroyed five hostile forces. On August 6 he marched into Caracas at the front of his army and freed the city. Given the title of "Liberator," he appointed himself military dictator. His hold on the city, however, did not last. Spanish forces recaptured Caracas in 1814, forcing Bolívar to flee once again.

Surprise Attack Defeats Spanish

Exiled in Jamaica in September 1815, Bolívar wrote his famous *La Carte de Jamaica* (The Letter from Jamaica). In it, he called for republican governments, like that of England, to be set up throughout South America. For the next two years, supported by the government in Haiti, Bolívar led several invasions of Venezuela, but most failed. He finally returned to Venezuela in 1817 and secured command of the revolutionary army. After a few victories, he gained the support of José Antonio Páez, leader of the fierce fighting *llaneros* (Venezuelan plainsmen). Bolívar decided to surprise the main Spanish force in present-day Colombia by crossing the Andes Mountains and attacking from the rear. His plan worked. On August 7, 1819, he decisively defeated the Spanish at Boyacá. In December he was made president of Greater Colombia (present-day Colombia, Venezuela, Panama, and Ecuador).

The republic of Greater Colombia initially existed only on paper, but Bolívar soon made it real. By June 1821 Venezuela was officially free. The following May Ecuador was liberated. Two years later Peru gained its freedom. The revolution of South America came to a close in April 1825 when the last Spanish forces on the continent were driven from *Alto Perú* (Upper Peru). This new nation celebrated its freedom on August 6 by choosing to be called Bolivia, after the Liberator of South America.

Making these free South American republics into a strong confederation was not an easy task for Bolívar. In 1826 he tried to bring together in Panama representatives from all the nations in the Americas. Only Colombia, Peru, Central America, and Mexico attended and signed a treaty of alliance. But this meeting marked the beginning of Pan-Americanism, a movement of political and economic cooperation between the nations of North, Central, and South America that continues to this day.

Bolívar had freed his fellow South Americans from Spanish rule, but they did not share his dream of a confederation. Constant revolts flared up in the republics against unity and his strict rule. Trying to stop the confederation from cracking, he declared himself dictator on September 24, 1828. The next night he barely escaped assassination. The end of Greater Colombia, though, was unavoidable. In the fall of 1829, Venezuela and Ecuador seceded and the confederation was over. In poor health, Bolívar resigned the presidency in 1830, dying of tuberculosis soon afterward.

William Bradford

Governor of Plymouth Colony

Born in March 1590,
Austerfield, Yorkshire, England

Died May 9, 1657,
Plymouth Colony

"More than anyone, Bradford is responsible for the survival of Plymouth Colony."

I n September of 1620 a group of 102 men and women, most seeking religious freedom, crowded on a small ship and journeyed from Plymouth, England, to America. They sailed over the treacherous waters of the North Atlantic for two months before arriving in present-day Massachusetts. But this group of people, known to American history as the Pilgrims, were unprepared for the wild land to which they had come. Half of them, including the governor of the colony, died that first winter. The following spring those who remained elected a new leader, a 30-year-old named William Bradford. He would be reelected 30 more times and would lead his people through years of hardship and of success. More than anyone, he is responsible for the survival of Plymouth Colony.

Hardly anything is known about Bradford's childhood. His father died a year after he was born, followed by his mother six years later. Different relatives then took turns raising the young Bradford. At the age of 12 he joined a local Puritan church, a bold act for someone of his young age. The Puritans disagreed strongly with the English government's control over the Church of England, and they thought all Roman Catholic customs still used in the Church should be removed. Many of the English persecuted the Puritans for these beliefs.

In 1606 Bradford joined a new group of Puritans called Separatists. As their name implies, they wanted to separate from the Church of England rather than to reform it. Because of this, they faced even harsher criticism, and in 1608 they moved to Holland with hopes of finding more religious toleration. Bradford went along and, after a few years there, married Dorothy May. But Bradford and many of the Separatists soon felt they were losing their English heritage by staying in Holland, and in 1620 they decided to move to America. After receiving permission from the Virginia Company of London, which held the rights to colonize the territory around present-day Virginia, they boarded the *Mayflower*. On September 16 they set sail on a pilgrimage across the Atlantic.

Landing at Plymouth Bay

Their destination was Virginia, but on November 21 they arrived off the coast of present-day Cape Cod, Massachusetts. They spent the next month exploring the shoreline before finally landing at Plymouth Bay on December 26. Because they were outside of the domain of the Virginia Company, the Pilgrims needed a form of civil government. They composed the Mayflower Compact, the first written constitution in America. Even though they continued to pledge allegiance to the king of England, the Pilgrims governed themselves with elected leaders.

The first winter at Plymouth Colony was brutal. While many Pilgrims died from exposure to the weather, others died from scurvy, a disease caused by a lack of vitamin C. Among the dead were Bradford's wife and Governor John Carver. In the spring, the Pilgrims elected Bradford governor. He was now responsible for administering justice, for keeping records of overseas trading, and for negotiating treaties with Native American tribes.

The Pilgrims' situation improved when they met an English-speaking Pawtuxet named Squanto, who had been taken

Thanksgiving Day

By order of Governor William Bradford, the first Thanksgiving was a three-day festival. The Pilgrims and the surrounding Native Americans gathered to eat and to compete in games. Although thanksgivings were held after this, a national Thanksgiving Day holiday was not celebrated in America for over two hundred years. In 1863 Abraham Lincoln declared the last Thursday in November as a national harvest celebration. This date, however, had to be proclaimed yearly by the president and by the governor of each state. Finally, in 1941, Congress passed a resolution making the fourth Thursday of November a national legal holiday.

to England in 1615 and had remained there for a few years. He taught the Pilgrims how to preserve fish and how to plant corn. He also helped Bradford sign a peace treaty with Massasoit, the chief of the local Wampanoag tribe. Grateful for the harvest they reaped that year, the Pilgrims held a thanksgiving feast of venison, wild turkey, and corn in the autumn of 1621.

Pilgrims Suffer First Few Years

The second winter was equally harsh. Supplies did not arrive from England and Bradford had to ration out food to the Pilgrims. Squanto died from smallpox, a disease the Pilgrims had brought with them from Europe. Bradford was forced to lead several expeditions along the Massachusetts coast to trade for food with other Native American tribes. More settlers soon arrived from England, but they brought very little food with them and the constant threat of starvation lasted for several years.

The soil around Plymouth Colony was poor, and many Pilgrims eventually pushed northward, claiming and settling on more productive land owned by native tribes. Bradford managed the Pilgrims' growing fur trade, and by 1627 he had enough money to repay the London merchants who had backed the *Mayflower*'s trip. Bradford accepted almost all new settlers into Plymouth Colony, but he was smart enough to banish those swindlers and trouble-makers who came merely to take advantage of the Pilgrims. Because of his foresight and leadership, the colony soon grew into a dozen different towns all along the Cape Cod area.

Bradford began writing his *History of Plymouth Plantation* in 1630 and worked on it the rest of his life. At the beginning of his book he described the Native Americans as savages, wild beasts, and cannibals. But as the years passed, his prejudice decreased as his understanding grew, and by the end of the book he wrote of them with respect. Bradford was a devout Puritan throughout his time at Plymouth Colony. Although he had helped the colony flourish, he believed in his later years that it had moved away from the original religious ideals on which it had been founded. On May 9, 1657, he died quietly in his home.

Samuel de Champlain

French explorer, founder of Quebec

Born c. 1570,
Brouage, France

Died December 25, 1635,
Quebec, New France, present-day Canada

"Because Samuel de Champlain had a strong vision that saw beyond the simple trade for furs, he is considered the chief founder of New France and Canada."

Throughout the sixteenth century, English, Dutch, and French explorers searched for a trade route by water that would quickly lead to East Asia and its riches of spices and silks. They sailed around the upper part of the North American continent looking for such a route, which they called the Northwest Passage. They discovered no such natural passage, only the rich, virgin lands of present-day eastern Canada. Although they did not make it to East Asia, they found wealth by fishing the surrounding waters and by trading for furs with the Native Americans they encountered. French explorers claimed the rich lands around the Gulf of St. Lawrence for their king and called it "New France."

These explorers did not set up colonies, however, only temporary trading posts. This changed with the arrival of Samuel de Champlain. He came to New France as a member of a fur-trading expedition, but spent his time exploring the unknown lands in the region. In 1608 he founded the settlement of Quebec and struggled for almost the next thirty years to keep his dream of a permanent colony alive. Because he had a strong vision that saw beyond the simple trade for furs, he is considered the chief founder of New France and Canada.

Champlain was born around 1570 to Antoine de Complain [sic] and Margueritte Le Roy. Very few records exist about his early life. It is believed that his desire to sail the oceans was fueled by his father, a naval captain, and by the other sailors in his hometown of Brouage, a French seaport on the Bay of Biscay. In 1598 he went to Spain and embarked on a three-year voyage to the West Indies and Central America. He became an excellent draftsman and geographer, and when he returned to France he was invited on a fur-trading expedition to New France in 1603. On this short-lived journey he explored the St. Lawrence River as far west as present-day Montreal, drawing maps and gathering information about the region.

Explores Nova Scotia

Champlain sailed back to New France in 1604 with Pierre du Gua de Monts, who had been awarded control of the fur trade in the area by French king Henry IV. Together the men scouted Nova Scotia and New Brunswick. The following summer they continued their explorations, this time as far south as present-day Cape Cod, Massachusetts. From these trips, Champlain drew the first detailed maps of New England. Their camp at Port-Royal (Annapolis Royal, Nova Scotia) lasted through two harsh winters, but had to be abandoned when the king canceled Monts's trade monopoly.

Champlain and Monts returned to New France in 1608, but this time they sailed up the St. Lawrence River to the site of present-day Quebec. Here Champlain established the first year-round white settlement in Canada. The initial purpose of Quebec was to promote fur trade with the Native Americans. The French were on good terms with the Algonquin, Montagnais, and Huron tribes, and Champlain helped them in their combined war against the Iroquois. In the spring of 1609 he and French troops traveled with Huron warriors to present-day upper New York state to fight the Iroquois. There he discovered the large lake that bears his name today.

Champlain went to France late in 1610 to help Monts secure trading rights from the new king, Louis XIII, and financial backing from independent merchants. Before returning to New France he married the 12-year-old Hélène Boullé. Over the next few years he explored areas west of Quebec and established a trading post at Mount Royal (present-day Montreal). In 1615, accompanied by a few Huron, Champlain went as far west as Georgian Bay on Lake Huron, then journeyed back to Quebec by way of Lake Ontario in the southeast. Wounded while again helping the Huron fight the Iroquois, he had to spend that winter with them.

Builds Up Quebec Colony

Champlain did no more exploring after this, devoting himself, instead, to the Quebec colony. He proposed to Louis XIII that if the king supported Quebec as a formal colony, France would receive the wealth from the natural resources in the area and the settlers in the colony would be subject to the king's laws. Louis XIII agreed to Champlain's plan and made him administrator of Quebec. Champlain built up the colony and tried to establish better relations with the surrounding tribes, including the Iroquois. He adopted two Native American girls, whom he named Hope and Charity. In time, though, he wanted more political influence over the tribes, even insisting on his own choice of chiefs.

The settlers at Quebec were poor farmers and continued to be dependent on France for supplies. In 1628 the English attacked settlements around Quebec and soon demanded that the colony be given to them. The French refused, but the English intercepted supplies headed for Quebec and the colonists almost starved. In July of 1629 Champlain had to surrender the colony. He was taken to England as a prisoner for a short while before being released. The English finally gave Quebec back to the French after the two countries signed the Treaty of Saint-Germain-en-Laye in 1632. Champlain returned to Quebec for the last time in May of 1633 and spent the next two and a half years strengthening the colony. He died there on Christmas Day, 1635.

Chief Joseph

Nez Percé leader
Born 1840
Died 1905

The story of Chief Joseph and his band of Nez Percé sadly depicts the poor treatment of Native Americans by the American government in the late 1800s. The Nez Percé lived in the Wallowa Valley, a mountainous region on the boundaries of Idaho, Oregon, and Washington. Warfare had been a way of life for them and their neighboring tribes for centuries. With the American government, however, the Nez Percé—led by Chief Joseph—tried repeatedly to avoid conflict. A series of broken promises and false treaties on the part of the government forced the Nez Percé into a war and resulted in the removal of the tribe from their homeland. For the last 28 years of his life, Chief Joseph pleaded with the government to let his people return to their way of life. His calm and eloquent pleas went unheard.

The Nez Percé people belonged to the Shahaptian tribal family. They were traditional enemies of the Shoshone, Bannock, and Paiute tribes of the Great Basin region to their south and east. They were given the name of Nez Percé ("pierced

"His calm and eloquent pleas went unheard."

nose") by the French because some of the tribal members decorated their noses with shells or pendants. They herded animals, lived off wild plants, and fished for salmon in the mountain rivers. When the horse was introduced into their culture around 1700, they began hunting for buffalo and traveling farther for trade. They met white men for the first time in 1805 when the famous explorers Lewis and Clark passed through their territory and befriended them. After this, the Nez Percé increased their contact with white men. It proved to be their downfall.

In the 1830s, religious missionaries (teachers who try to convert others to different religious beliefs) came to the Pacific Northwest region. Old Joseph, father of the future chief, was given a Christian wedding just before the birth of his son in 1840. A missionary named the baby Ephraim and raised him as a Christian. But he was also named Hin-mah-too-yah-lat-kekht and learned traditional tribal lore from his family.

Over the next ten years the Nez Percé's territory was permanently changed. The number of white settlers using the Oregon Trail to head west each year grew from only a handful to thousands. By 1855, white politicians tried to convince the Nez Percé tribes to give up their lands. And by the 1860s, when gold was discovered in the region, pressure on the Nez Percé increased dramatically. Some branches of the Nez Percé signed their lands over to the government, but Old Joseph did not. Angered by the white invasion and by what they thought was a false treaty, Old Joseph and his son declared they were no longer Christians.

Government Withdraws Treaty

Young Joseph became chief of his band of Nez Percé in 1871 when his father died. A treaty with the government in 1873 confirmed his people's right to the Wallowa Valley. Yet the government reversed its decision just two years later and let white settlers into the valley. Chief Joseph resisted going to war. He convinced the local U.S. Army commander, General Oliver Otis Howard, that the Nez Percé were justified in their claims to their land. But in 1877 Howard was forced to follow the commands of an unsympathetic army leader. He ordered Chief Joseph to move his group to a reservation at Lapwai, Idaho, a day's ride away by horse.

As the Nez Percé approached the reservation, a member of Joseph's band, Wahlitits, killed four white settlers who were known as Indian-haters. He sought revenge for his father who had been killed by settlers several years earlier. This was the spark that ignited the war Chief Joseph had tried to avoid. From June to October of 1877, the Nez Percé fought with and ran from government troops. At one point, Chief Joseph led his band into Yellowstone, Wyoming, which had been designated a national park just five years earlier. Far from their homes, the Nez Percé were lost. They finally found a way out of the park and headed north to Canada. Forty miles short of the border, government troops surrounded the Nez Percé and, after a week-long battle in freezing conditions, forced them to surrender.

His People Denied Their Homeland

Throughout most of the Nez Percé's long flight, Joseph's main task was to care for his band's children, old people, and animals, rather than to fight. The army officer who captured the Nez Percé, Colonel Nelson Miles, recognized this when he and Joseph met to discuss the conditions of surrender. Impressed by the intelligence of Chief Joseph and his people, Miles agreed to let the band return to Idaho. But the government would not let Miles keep his promise. The Nez Percé were taken, instead, to Bismarck, North Dakota, and then to Fort Leavenworth, Kansas. In this flat and swampy area, so different from their homeland, many Nez Percé contracted malaria and died. They were finally moved to an equally unhealthy reservation in Oklahoma.

Chief Joseph began pleading with the government to let the Nez Percé return to the Wallowa Valley. He wrote letters to the Bureau of Indian Affairs, to the many army officers he had befriended, and to the president. Nothing worked. He began making public speeches, and even wrote an article for the *North American Review* in which he justified his people's conduct. Joseph's arguments detailing his band's poor situation convinced many Americans, but not those in power. In 1885 the government allowed the Nez Percé to return to the Pacific Northwest, yet only to a reservation and not to their homeland in Wallowa Valley. Chief Joseph died in 1905 still trying to convince the government to fulfill its treaty obligations.

Crazy Horse

Oglala Sioux chief
Born 1841
Died September 5, 1877

The Oregon Trail ran west along the Platte River across present-day Nebraska and Wyoming. Beginning around 1840, pioneers in wagon trains followed this route to final destinations in present-day California and Oregon. Within five years, over 3,000 white settlers were traveling the trail yearly. They brought with them hopes of finding gold and of starting a new life in the western wilderness. Like their European ancestors, they also brought with them diseases. Exposure to the whites was devastating for Crazy Horse's people, the Oglala Sioux. Their land, their health, and their way of life were destroyed. A passionate hater of the whites, Crazy Horse spent his life fighting them. He was a proud warrior, but his victories against the whites could not stop the eventual destruction of his people.

Crazy Horse had been exposed to whites from a very young age. Born in 1841, he was raised close to the Oregon Trail. When he was eight years old, a cholera epidemic swept through the Oglala tribe. The following year, an outbreak of

"Crazy Horse was a proud warrior, but his victories against the whites could not stop the eventual destruction of his people."

smallpox was equally damaging. Crazy Horse, who had grown up strong, escaped contracting these diseases. When he was a child, he had a vision of a warrior who could not be killed. Taking this as a sign, he trained to become a warrior. He killed his first buffalo when he was ten and his first human (a woman of the Omaha tribe) when he was fourteen. He quickly developed the prized accomplishments of the Oglala: skill with horses and weapons and bravery in battle.

In raids against rival tribes, Crazy Horse was fearless and lucky. He rode into battle with a lightening bolt painted across his face and hail stones painted on his upper body. He believed he would never be harmed as long as he followed his visions, which directed him to fight in front of his fellow warriors and to never retreat. His hunting parties were almost always successful. But like most other Native Americans of the Great Plains, he made the mistake of continuing to fight against his traditional rivals, instead of uniting against their common white enemy.

Whites Invade Sacred Black Hills

At the end of the Civil War in 1865, white migration westward increased and new trails were opened. The Sioux were especially outraged by the Bozeman Trail, named for John Bozeman, a white guide. A shortcut for miners heading into Montana, this trail cut along the eastern slopes of the Black Hills in present-day South Dakota—country sacred to all Sioux. Red Cloud, leader of the Sioux, swore in 1866 that he would never negotiate with the whites until the trail and all forts along it were closed.

Angry over the white invasion of sacred land, Crazy Horse led hundreds of Oglala warriors against Fort Phil Kearney on the Bozeman Trail. On December 21, 1866, he and a small group lured Captain William Fetterman and 80 of his troops out of the fort. The remaining warriors then ambushed the troops in what came to be known as the Fetterman massacre. The Oglala killed all of the soldiers and mutilated their bodies as a warning to other whites.

During the next two years, Crazy Horse and Red Cloud continually attacked army forts along the trail. Finally, in late

1868, the army abandoned the trail and the forts, which the Sioux burned to the ground. The U.S. government then offered to sign the Fort Laramie Treaty, a peace treaty that established a huge Sioux reservation in all of the Dakotas west of the Missouri River. Red Cloud and other Sioux chiefs agreed to the treaty and settled on the reservation. Crazy Horse and Sitting Bull (see **Sitting Bull**), chief of the Hunkpapa Sioux, refused to honor the treaty and settled with a few Sioux tribes west of the reservation.

The Black Hills were part of the reservation, but when gold was discovered there in 1875, miners flooded in. The U.S. government quickly sought to renegotiate the treaty to obtain either the land or the mineral rights, but the Sioux chiefs declined. In response, the government threatened the Sioux with warfare if all the Sioux tribes did not move to the reservation. Sitting Bull then united the Sioux who had refused the treaty with the neighboring Cheyenne and Arapaho.

Leads Warriors at Little Bighorn

In previous years, the Native Americans could not soundly defeat the U.S. Army because they did not organize their attacks. This time they did. When the army marched into the territory west of the reservation in 1876, the combined native forces were ready. Crazy Horse defeated General George Crook and his forces on the Rosebud River on June 17. A week later, at the battle of the Little Bighorn, Crazy Horse led the native forces in their slaughter of General George Armstrong Custer and the Seventh Cavalry. The tribes had to separate after this battle because of a shortage of food for men and horses. The advantage they had was lost.

Crazy Horse spent the following months raiding mining camps in the Black Hills and killing as many of the invading miners as he could find. He soon faced a new opponent, Colonel Nelson Miles, and for the first time he had to retreat. Miles recognized that the Native Americans fought only in summer, so he attacked in the winter. Although Crazy Horse and his warriors fought off Miles and his troops in January 1877, their camp and supplies were ruined. By spring, Crazy

Horse and his 1,000 followers faced starvation. Reluctantly, they surrendered at the Red Cloud government agency in present-day northwest Nebraska.

Relations among the many chiefs at the agency were uneasy. Those who had been there for many years thought Crazy Horse might try to lead a rebellion. They had him arrested on September 5, 1877. As he was being led to the guardhouse, however, a scuffle broke out. Crazy Horse was fatally stabbed, either by a soldier or by a native rival. His death only saved the great warrior from witnessing the end of his people's traditional way of life on the Great Plains.

Frederick Douglass

Leading American abolitionist

*Born in February 1818,
near Easton, Maryland*

*Died February 20, 1895,
Washington, D.C.*

Since he had lived the first 20 years of his life as a slave, Frederick Douglass knew the horrors of slavery. After he had taught himself to read and to write, he escaped to freedom. He joined the abolitionist (antislavery) movement and told the gripping story of his early life. He became an influential newspaper editor and, more important, one of the most distinguished and effective orators of his time. He met with presidents to lobby for the recognition of black rights, and he was not above criticizing them for what he saw as a lack of action. Douglass did not limit his fight to the inequalities of black Americans, but objected to every sign of discrimination—social, racial, and sexual. Believing the power to vote was the power of freedom, he was equally active in the woman suffrage (right to vote) movement.

Douglass was born Frederick Augustus Washington Bailey sometime in February 1818. Both he and his mother, Harriet Bailey, were slaves of Captain Aaron Anthony. No one was quite sure who his white father was. While still an infant,

"Douglass did not limit his fight to the inequalities of black Americans, but objected to every sign of discrimination—social, racial, and sexual."

Douglass was separated from his mother and raised by his grandmother. In 1825 he became a servant to Anthony's daughter, Sophia, and her husband Hugh Auld. Over the next 13 years, Douglass worked in stores or on farms in Maryland for relatives of the Aulds or others who rented him. Many of these owners treated him poorly; some beat him every day.

Sophia Auld had begun to teach the young Douglass how to read. Although her husband quickly put an end to these teachings, Douglass had learned enough to continue his own education. At the age of 13, with money he earned from shining shoes, he bought *The Columbian Orator,* which contained many essays and speeches about human freedom. This book, his first, had a lasting impact on Douglass—he quoted passages from it throughout his life.

The immediate effect of this book was Douglass's rising desire to experience the freedom he could only read about. In 1835, while rented out to farmer William Freeland, Douglass began secretly to teach free blacks and other slaves how to read. He also planned to escape with five other slaves by stealing a boat and sailing up the Chesapeake Bay, then following the North Star on foot to Philadelphia. Before they could act, their plan was discovered and they were all jailed. Douglass was returned to Hugh Auld and then sent to work in the shipyards in Baltimore.

Still determined to escape from bondage, Douglass worked and waited. On September 3, 1838, disguised in sailor's clothes, he rode a train to New York. For the time being, he was free. He married Anna Murray, a free black whom he had courted in Baltimore. They settled in New Bedford, Massachusetts, where he worked as a common laborer—shoveling coal, digging cellars, and sawing wood. He changed his surname to Douglass, based on the heroine in the poem "The Lady of the Lake" by the English Romantic poet Sir Walter Scott.

Joins Abolitionists After Passionate Speech

In 1841, while attending a meeting of the Massachusetts Anti-Slavery Society, Douglass delivered a speech about his

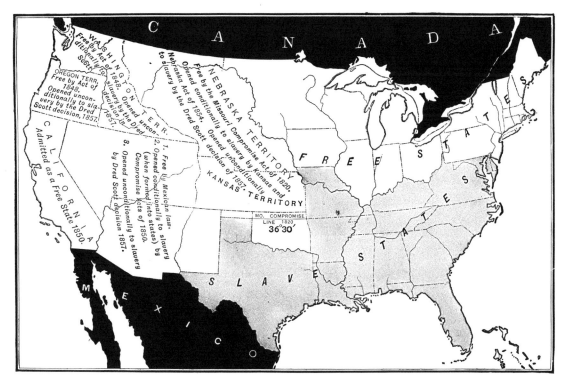

AREA OF FREEDOM AND SLAVERY IN 1857.

early life. Though he stammered at the beginning, he was so effective by the end that the audience cheered him wildly. Abolitionist leader William Lloyd Garrison, who had been in the audience, was so impressed that he asked Douglass to join the Massachusetts Society as a full-time speaker. Douglass agreed. Though mobbed and beaten in towns where he spoke, Douglass endured and quickly became one of the nation's leading abolitionists.

Because Douglass was intelligent and spoke English eloquently, many people doubted he was ever a slave. In response, he wrote his autobiography, *Narrative of the Life of Frederick Douglass,* published in 1845. The honesty and vividness of the writing removed all doubts about his story. By revealing his real name and his various owners as a slave, however, Douglass risked being recaptured. He immediately went to England for two years, hoping through his speeches to increase support for the American abolitionist movement.

While there, he raised enough money to buy his permanent freedom from his last owner.

After returning to America in 1847, Douglass moved to Rochester, New York, and started a weekly newspaper, *North Star* (called *Frederick Douglass's Paper* after 1851). Although devoted mainly to antislavery, the paper also supported the causes of black education and woman suffrage. While Garrison and members of his American Anti-Slavery Society thought that moral arguments were the best way to end slavery, Douglass did not. He called for direct political action and even encouraged black violence. Because of their differing opinions, the two men split in 1851.

Douglass became increasingly outspoken. In 1855 he published *My Bondage and My Freedom,* a revision of his autobiography. The following year he started meeting with the fiery abolitionist John Brown. He agreed with Brown's idea of a slave rebellion, but did not support Brown's plan to seize the federal arsenal at Harpers Ferry, Maryland, in November 1859. Even so, after Brown's raid failed, Douglass feared he might be arrested as an accomplice. He fled to Canada and then traveled back to England where he lectured for six months.

Urges Lincoln to Draft Black Soldiers

After the start of the Civil War in 1861, Douglass urged U.S. President Abraham Lincoln to make the end of slavery the main goal of the war. When Lincoln did not act quickly on this matter, Douglass openly criticized him. Lincoln, however, recognized the importance of Douglass's input and twice called him to the White House for conferences. Throughout the war, Douglass supported the use of black troops to help the Union cause. When two black Massachusetts regiments were finally created in 1863, two of Douglass's sons were among the first recruits.

During the 12 years of Reconstruction that followed the end of the Civil War, Douglass pushed for civil and voting rights for blacks. In 1868 he saw Congress pass the Fourteenth Amendment, which recognized the citizenship of all people born in America. Two years later, Congress ratified the Fifteenth

Amendment, extending voting rights to all black males. Even though this amendment did not give women the right to vote, Douglass supported it. Many women criticized him for this.

Douglass spent his last years in civil service positions. Beginning in 1877, he served as the U.S. Marshal for the District of Columbia. Then in 1881, U.S. President James A. Garfield gave him the post of Recorder of Deeds for the district. That same year he published the last version of his autobiography, *The Life and Times of Frederick Douglass*. For the rest of his life he continued speaking out on black civil rights and other issues of inequality. In 1884, two years after his first wife's death, he married Helen Pitts, his white secretary. Douglass died of a heart attack on February 25, 1895, having just returned from a woman suffrage convention.

W. E. B. Du Bois

Founder of the National Association for the Advancement of Colored People (NAACP)

Born February 23, 1868,
Great Barrington, Massachusetts

Died August 27, 1963,
Accra, Ghana

"For his efforts to achieve racial equality, Du Bois is recognized as a pioneer of the American civil rights movement."

While growing up in Massachusetts, William Edward Burghardt Du Bois never knew racial discrimination. His intelligence earned him the friendship and respect of his mostly white classmates. When he attended Fisk University in Tennessee in the 1880s, however, he came face to face with the South's system of racial segregation. Jim Crow laws set up rigid divisions between blacks and whites in public places. Frightened by these restrictions, Du Bois never rode a streetcar or went to a movie theater. His experiences at Fisk led him to devote his education to the study of the social problems facing African Americans. Increasing racism in America in the early twentieth century soon led him to devote his life to the struggle for African American freedom. For his efforts to achieve racial equality, Du Bois is recognized as a pioneer of the American civil rights movement.

Du Bois was born in 1868 in the rural New England village of Great Barrington, Massachusetts. His mother, Mary Burghardt Du Bois, had been abandoned by her husband and was forced to raise her son alone. The young Du Bois excelled in school and helped support his family by working odd jobs—splitting wood, shoveling coal, selling tea at the local A & P store.

Du Bois had wanted to enroll in Harvard University, but lacked the money to attend. Instead, he went to Fisk. After three years in the hostile environment there, Du Bois seized the chance to transfer to Harvard. He completed his undergraduate studies in 1888 and went on to receive his master of arts degree in 1891. He spent the following two years studying and traveling abroad. Upon his return in 1895, he obtained his doctorate from Harvard, becoming the first African American to receive that degree from the university. He spent most of the next fifteen years teaching economics and history at Atlanta University. In 1896 he married Nina Gomer, and they stayed together until her death in 1950.

Writes First Studies of African Americans

Out of the classroom, Du Bois devoted his time to writing and research. In 1899 he published *The Philadelphia Negro,* the first study of an African American community ever undertaken. His most significant work on African American life, however, was published four years later. *The Souls of Black Folk* documented the abuse of African Americans since the Civil War. Although Du Bois had hoped his logical arguments would convince white Americans of the need for racial justice, the book did little to stop the rising racial violence in America. At that time, on average, one African American continued to be lynched (hanged) every other day.

Du Bois soon believed only protest could bring about change. In 1905 he founded the Niagara Movement, the first African American organization that demanded total equality. By taking this stand, the Movement openly disagreed with the policies of the influential African American leader Booker T. Washington (see **Booker T. Washington**), who called only for economic equality. In 1910, along with others, Du Bois transformed the Niagara Movement into the interracial National Association for the Advancement of Colored People (NAACP).

W.E.B. Du Bois (left) at an NAACP ceremony

He gave up his teaching position to become editor of the NAACP journal *The Crisis,* a post he held for the next 24 years. His editorials shocked many people. He attacked the idea of democracy in America and urged African Americans to resort to violence if necessary to protect themselves.

Radical Views Upset NAACP Leaders

Du Bois's concern for black freedom soon extended beyond America. In 1919 in Paris, France, he helped organize the first of several Pan-African Congresses. This congress adopted resolutions calling for the independence of former German colonies in Africa and for the humane treatment of all Africans. When the rest of the world paid little attention to these resolutions, Du Bois returned to America more determined to fight for his cause. His writings in *The Crisis* became more radical. He promoted the idea that African Americans could achieve freedom only by having separate economic, social, and political organizations. Because of his controversial beliefs, Du Bois was forced to resign as editor of *The Crisis* in 1934.

Du Bois returned to Atlanta University to teach for ten years. During the latter 1930s, he urged African Americans to support democratic movements that would gain Africans independence throughout the world. By the mid-1940s, however, Du Bois began supporting policies of the communist Soviet Union. In 1949 he attended a peace conference in Moscow, and in 1951 he circulated a petition in America to ban nuclear weapons. He was arrested and tried by the federal government for being an agent of the Soviet Union. Although the charge against the 83-year-old Du Bois was dropped, the government continued to harass him. His books were seized and many of his speeches were canceled. His passport was confiscated in 1952 and he could not travel outside the country for six years.

When the civil rights movement grew in America in the late 1950s, many African Americans looked to Du Bois as a leader. Nonetheless, the NAACP refused to accept him because of his political views. By this time, he had come to embrace communism, which he believed stood for national freedom and peace. On October 1, 1961, he joined the United States Communist party. Four days later, at the invitation of Ghana President Kwame Nkrumah, Du Bois left to live in that west African country. He never returned to America, dying in Ghana on August 27, 1963.

Benjamin Franklin

American statesman, writer, inventor, printer

Born January 17, 1706,
Boston, Massachusetts

Died April 17, 1790,
Philadelphia, Pennsylvania

> *"Franklin quickly learned ... to be thrifty and hard working, and these traits carried him through the many phases of his life."*

Benjamin Franklin was not lucky enough to receive a formal education or to inherit money from his family. Born the fifteenth child in a family of seventeen children, he received only two years of schooling. Working hard and being thrifty were traits that carried him through the many phases of his life. In business he was successful enough to retire at age 42. He then focused on inventions and scientific experiments, earning international recognition for his achievements. He devoted the remainder of his long life to politics and diplomacy, becoming a leader in the call for American rights. By the time he died in 1790, he was one of the most admired men in the world.

Franklin was born in 1706 in Boston to Josiah and Abiah Franklin. He started working in his father's tallow shop when he was ten, making candles and soap. He hated the work, though, and two years later agreed to work as an apprentice to his older brother James, a printer. He became almost an expert under James's teaching, and for the rest of his life always referred to himself as a printer. During his five-year apprenticeship, Franklin educated himself by reading anything he could find. He also began his lifelong career as a writer by secretly submitting articles to the *New England Courant,* a newspaper published by James.

Franklin moved to Philadelphia in 1723. Over the next six years he developed his printing skills further by working in shops in Philadelphia and in London, England. He saved enough money by 1729 to purchase the almost bankrupt *Pennsylvania Gazette.* Through hard work, he increased the newspaper's circulation and made a high profit. On September 1, 1730, he took Deborah Read as his common-law wife. (They never officially married because she never divorced her first husband who had deserted her.)

The 1730s were busy and productive years for Franklin. He started writing and publishing *Poor Richard's Almanack* in 1732, and it made him famous throughout the 13 colonies. Many people identified with the character of Poor Richard Saunders and his common sense sayings, such as "Haste makes Waste," "Eat to live, and not live to eat," and "Fish and Visitors stink after three days." In addition to business, Franklin put his energies into social projects in Philadelphia. He founded police and fire forces, and suggested that the city's streets be paved and lighted, advanced ideas for the time. He established what many consider the first circulating library in America and an academy that later became the University of Pennsylvania. In 1736 he was appointed to his first political position, clerk of the Pennsylvania Assembly (legislature), a position he held for the next 15 years.

Flies a Kite During a Thunderstorm

The wealth Franklin earned from his *Almanack* and other business ventures allowed him to pursue his scientific interests during the 1740s and early 1750s. He invented such useful items as the Franklin stove, bifocal lenses, and the lightening rod. The study of electricity was particularly interesting to him. His famous kite-flying experiment during a thunderstorm proved that electricity existed in lightening. For his scientific

Benjamin Franklin returns from one of his many trips to Europe.

studies, Franklin received honorary master of arts degrees from Harvard, Yale, and the College of William and Mary, and an honorary doctorate from Oxford in England. These awards pleased him more than any others he received in his life.

After retiring from business in 1748, Franklin devoted himself entirely to politics. He was appointed deputy postmaster general of the colonies in 1753 and helped reorganize the postal service to make it more efficient. He attended the Albany Congress in 1754, where representatives of seven colonies decided how they would stand on the recently begun French and Indian War, which pitted England against France over land claims in America. During the session Franklin offered a plan to unite the 13 colonies. Although it was not adopted, parts of the plan were used later in state and national constitutions.

Franklin traveled to England in 1757 as the colonial representative for Pennsylvania. Within a few years, three more colonies had chosen him as their agent. Except for two years (1762-64), Franklin spent most of his adult life in England, becoming the London-based "spokesman" for America. In his dealings with English officials, he was a moderate and cautious diplomat and earned the respect of all. He became more outspoken, however, with the passage of the Stamp Act in 1765. Hoping to raise money to support its army in America, England required a stamp (a tax) to be placed on all newspapers, legal documents, and other business papers sold in the colonies. This was the first time England had ever taxed anything within the borders of the colonies, and Americans revolted. Through his eloquent arguing, Franklin forced Parliament, England's law-making body, to repeal the Stamp Act in 1766.

Leads Call for American Independence

Because of his stand on the Stamp Act, Franklin's relations with English officials soured. A movement protesting English rule had been growing in the colonies, and Franklin now became a leader in the call for complete independence. He returned to Philadelphia in May of 1775, just after the beginning of the American Revolution, and was immediately chosen to be a member of the Second Continental Congress. Along with Thomas Jefferson (see **Thomas Jefferson**) and John Adams, Franklin served on a committee to draft the Declaration of Independence the following June. Although written mainly by Jefferson, the Declaration contained many of Franklin's suggestions.

Franklin was appointed America's first minister to France in the autumn of 1776, and he sailed to that country seeking a treaty of alliance. He spent the next nine years there, and his wit and honest approach gained the friendship of both the government and the people of France. The treaty was signed on February 6, 1778, and the French aid secured by this treaty greatly helped the colonies in their struggle against England. Franklin then used his diplomatic skills to negotiate a peace settlement to end the American Revolution. On September 3, 1783, England signed the Treaty of Paris, formally recognizing America's independence.

After returning to America in 1785, the 79-year-old Franklin became president of the governing body of Pennsylvania. When the Constitutional Convention was held in Philadelphia in 1787, he served initially as a host and then as a full delegate. Even though he spoke only a few times during the sessions, he helped ease tensions during the often heated arguments between delegates. Although not satisfied with the completed Constitution of the United States, Franklin strongly urged all the delegates to sign the document. This was his last great public service. During the remaining years of his life, he worked to finish his *Autobiography,* which he had started in 1771. Though he did not complete the work (it covers only his early years), many consider it his best written piece. Franklin died quietly in the late evening of April 17, 1790.

Ulysses S. Grant

Eighteenth president of the United States and Union general during the American Civil War

*Born April 27, 1822,
Point Pleasant, Ohio*

*Died July 23, 1885,
Mount McGregor, New York*

The two main generals of the American Civil War—Ulysses S. Grant and Robert E. Lee (see **Robert E. Lee**)—could not have been greater opposites. Lee graduated at the top of his class from West Point and served honorably in the United States Army until the beginning of the Civil War. Grant, on the other hand, graduated in the middle of his class from West Point and remarked later that "a military life has no charms for me." He eventually resigned from the army and worked at a variety of jobs, all of them failures. Most historians even consider the two terms he served as president of the United States after the war as failures. His greatest career accomplishments came on the battlefield. Although Grant and Lee emerged from the Civil War as two great generals, Grant was the victor.

He was born Hiram Ulysses Grant in 1822 in a two-room log cabin in Pleasant Point, New York. His father, Jesse Grant, was a struggling tanner (person who works animal hides into leather). While growing up, Grant plowed fields and gathered

"Although Grant and Lee emerged from the Civil War as two great generals, Grant was the victor."

firewood on his father's farm. A sensitive and withdrawn boy, he preferred working with his father's horses and developed a life-long skill in handling them.

When he was 17, Grant reluctantly entered the United States Military Academy at West Point, New York. He had reversed his name to Ulysses Hiram Grant, but was mistakenly registered as Ulysses Simpson Grant (Simpson was his mother's maiden name). He simply accepted this name, and his friends at the academy called him Sam. An average student, he hated drills, parades, and the "spit-and-polish" of military dress. After his graduation in 1843 he did not get the cavalry duty he had wanted. Instead, he was assigned to army posts in Missouri, Louisiana, and Texas.

The Mexican War broke out in 1846 between the United States and Mexico over land claims in present-day southwestern United States. Grant was in Texas at the time, serving under General Zachary Taylor. Although he was a quartermaster (responsible for food, clothing, and equipment), Grant participated in several major battles and even led a charge. For his bravery, he received two citations and a promotion to the rank of first lieutenant. After the war ended in 1848, Grant married Julia Dent, and they eventually had three sons and a daughter.

Resigns from the Army

The army sent Grant to various posts from the Great Lakes to California, but did not allow his family to accompany him. Grant tried to raise money to bring them along, but his business ventures failed and his savings dried up. Lonely, he began drinking. Finally, in 1854, he resigned from the army. He began farming a piece of land his father-in-law gave him, but couldn't grow anything. He then tried bill collecting and real estate. Neither worked. He couldn't even sell firewood on the streets of St. Louis. He became so poor that he pawned his watch one Christmas in order to buy his family presents.

When the Civil War started in April 1861, Grant was working as a clerk in his father's leather store. He had no strong feelings about slavery, but he firmly believed in the

U.S. Grant and his generals at City Point, Virginia, the winter of 1864-65.

Union. The governor of Illinois appointed him colonel of the state's volunteer force. Four months later, he was appointed brigadier general. After a few insignificant battles, Grant captured Fort Donelson in Tennessee on February 16, 1862. The first major Union victory, it broke the Confederacy's hold on the West. Grant was made a major general. On April 6, however, he was badly surprised at the battle of Shiloh, named after a local church in southern Tennessee. The Union and

Confederate losses there totaled more than those of the American Revolution, the War of 1812, and the Mexican War combined. This two-day conflict came to be the most terrible battle of the entire war.

Many people called for Grant's removal after this, but U.S. President Abraham Lincoln refused to listen. Grant soon proved Lincoln right when he captured Vicksburg on July 4, 1863. Vicksburg, Mississippi, was a powerful fortress town on the Mississippi River. As long as the Confederates controlled this town, they controlled the flow of supplies on the river. After months of campaigns against the town and the surrounding area, Grant was victorious. With the Mississippi in Union hands, the Confederacy was cut in half and ultimately doomed.

Gains Command of Entire Union Force

Grant followed up this important victory by defeating the Confederates in November at the battle of Chattanooga, Tennessee. President Lincoln then named him supreme commander of the Union armies in March 1864. For the next year, Grant planned and carried out his final goal: the capture of the Confederate capital of Richmond, Virginia. He believed it was more important to destroy the enemy than to capture territory. He carried out his belief in the initial campaigns in Virginia— the Wilderness, Spotsylvania, and Cold Harbor were among the bloodiest battles ever seen. For nine months Grant lay siege to the city of Petersburg, just south of Richmond, protected by Confederate forces under Robert E. Lee. On April 2, 1865, the Confederate lines around the city gave way and Richmond lay open to attack.

The Civil War ended on April 9 when Lee surrendered to Grant at Appomattox Courthouse near Lynchburg, Virginia. Grant was generous in his peace terms. He allowed all the Confederate soldiers to return to their homes as long as they obeyed the laws. Moreover, he allowed them to keep their horses to use on their farms that spring. He also gave Lee 25,000 rations to help feed the near-starving Confederate troops.

In 1866 Grant was made a full general, a rank previously held in the U.S. Army only by George Washington. Grant soon disagreed with many of the policies of U.S. President Andrew Johnson and decided to run for the presidency himself as a member of the Republican party. Beginning in 1868, he was easily elected to two terms. Running the White House, however, proved to be a disaster for Grant. Politically unaware, he surrounded himself with dishonest politicians. Money scandals involved his vice president, his private secretary, his secretary of war, and people in the interior and navy departments.

After leaving office in 1877, Grant and his wife traveled around the world. He received great attention and praise everywhere he went. Upon his return to the United States, Grant settled in New York City and invested most his money in a Wall Street banking firm. This untrustworthy firm collapsed in 1884 and Grant was left bankrupt. That same year he was diagnosed with throat cancer. Determined to provide for his family, Grant signed a contract with his friend Mark Twain, the American writer, to publish his memoirs. In pain, he struggled to finish *The Personal Memoirs of U.S. Grant.* He completed the two-volume manuscript on July 16, 1885. One week later, Grant died. Sales of his work brought his family almost half a million dollars.

Ernesto "Ché" Guevara

Hero of the Cuban Revolution

*Born June 14, 1928,
Rosario, Argentina*

*Died October 9, 1967,
Higueras, Bolivia*

"To this day, Guevara remains a powerful symbol of Latin American and Third World revolution."

Raised in Argentina, Ernesto "Ché" Guevara trained to be a physician. His support for communism, however, led him throughout Central and South America seeking to help revolutionaries. In his travels, he met Cuban rebel Fidel Castro. Together they forged the Cuban Revolution that overthrew the government of that Caribbean island in the late 1950s. His interest in revolutions, however, was international, and he led rebellions in Africa and Bolivia. It was in the rugged jungles of this last country that he met his tragic end. His name was carried on by radical, young Americans of the late 1960s and early 1970s, who saw him as a champion against authority. To this day, Guevara remains a powerful symbol of Latin American and Third World revolution.

Guevara was born in 1928 in the city of Rosario in the Argentine province of Santa Fe. Both of his parents, Ernesto Guevara Lynch and Celia de la Serna, had come from wealthy families. As a result, Guevara grew up in comfortable surroundings. He suffered from severe asthma, however, and had to receive his early schooling at home. In the family library, he enjoyed reading the poetry of the Spaniard Federico García Lorca and the Chilean Pablo Neruda, both of whom were considered politically controversial. His mother also exposed him to the works of Karl Marx (see **Karl Marx**), the Prussian philosopher whose writings formed the basis of modern communism.

Partly because of his ill health, Guevara chose to become a doctor and entered the University of Buenos Aires in 1947. After completing his degree in 1953, he pursued revolutionary activities instead of medicine. He traveled throughout South and Central America before settling in Guatemala, where he worked for the pro-Communist President Jacobo Arbenz Guzmán. In May 1954, the Guatemalan military, backed by America's Central Intelligence Agency (CIA), seized control of the government. Guevara tried to organize a revolt against this takeover, but was unsuccessful. He sought refuge in the Argentine embassy in Guatemala for two months before escaping to Mexico.

Begins Life as a Revolutionary

This experience deepened Guevara's feelings against America. He believed armed struggle was now the only way to achieve social change in Latin America. This idea was supported by Hilda Gadea Acosta, who had become Guevara's companion in Guatemala. She encouraged him to fight for his revolutionary beliefs.

Guevara arrived in Mexico City in September 1954 and began working as a physician. Less than a year later, his life changed when he met Fidel Castro. The Cuban rebel planned to assemble a force and return to Cuba to overthrow Fulgencio Batista, a brutal dictator in Latin America. Guevara agreed to help Castro, becoming the only non-Cuban in his rebel force. After landing in Cuba on December 2, 1956, most of this force was wiped out in a battle with Batista's troops. The remaining 12 rebels, including Guevara and Castro, fled into the rugged Sierra Maestra mountains in eastern Cuba.

Over the next two years, these rebels fought the Revolution. An effective leader and fighter, Guevara served as second-in-command to Castro. His Cuban comrades began to call him "Ché," a warm Argentine expression meaning "you." The name stuck. Peasants from the surrounding countryside soon joined the rebels, whose guerrilla warfare—quick attacks and ambushes—proved successful. In late December 1959, Guevara led a band of rebels against a much larger Cuban army at the battle of Santa Clara in west-central Cuba. The rebel victory here forced Batista to flee the island on New Year's Eve. Four days later, Guevara and his band entered the capital city of Havana in triumph.

After Castro assumed control of the government, he made Guevara a citizen of Cuba. He then appointed Guevara president of the National Bank of Cuba. In this position, Guevara had to direct the economy. Prior to the Revolution, Cuba's main export was sugar and the largest market for it was America. Guevara sought to change that. In February 1960 he negotiated a trading pact with the Soviet Union. In exchange for sugar, the Soviets sent Cuba goods that could not be produced on the island. Trying to develop more trade relations, Guevara also traveled to other Communist countries. Beginning in 1961, he served as the minister of industries. He sought to reduce Cuba's emphasis on sugar and replace it with manufacturing industries. In addition, he tried to convince Cubans to work harder simply for the good of society.

Guevara, however, was a better revolutionary than an administrator. In 1960 he had published *Guerrilla Warfare,* a manual of guerrilla strategies and tactics. In this book, he openly stated that he hoped the Cuban victory would convince other revolutionaries to rise up in Latin America. Early in 1965 Guevara resigned his position in Cuba and dropped out of sight. For two years the general public knew nothing of his whereabouts.

Fought Secretly in Africa and Bolivia

It is now known that Guevara left Cuba to spread the idea of revolution. With over 100 Cuban rebels, he went to Africa to help overthrow the government of the Republic of the Congo (present-day Zaire). The poorly fought struggle soon disappointed Guevara, and he returned to Cuba after just six months. In October 1966 he secretly slipped into Bolivia disguised as an Uruguayan diplomat. Along with other Cuban guerrillas, he started a revolution that he hoped would expand into the surrounding countries of Peru, Brazil, Chili, Paraguay, and Argentina.

The rebellion in Bolivia proved even less successful than the one in the Congo. Guevara could not convince many of the peasants to join his cause. The harsh Bolivian jungles provided little food and many of his many men suffered from diseases such as malaria. Even so, the rebels continued their fight for almost a year. In late August 1967, however, Bolivian troops ambushed and killed one-half of Guevara's men. Without support, Guevara and the remaining rebels were finished. On October 8 the Bolivian army surrounded them in a canyon. In the fighting that followed, Guevara was seriously wounded and taken prisoner. Carried to the nearby town of Higueras, he was executed the next day.

Thomas Jefferson

President, philosopher, architect

Born April 13, 1743,
Albemarle County, Virginia

Died July 4, 1826,
at Monticello, central Virginia

"Except for minor changes by other committee members, Jefferson wrote the Declaration of Independence by himself."

So great were Thomas Jefferson's talents that even if he had not been involved in politics, his name would still be known to us. He was a scientist, a farmer, an architect, an engineer, a lawyer, a philosopher, and a writer. As a farmer, he experimented with seeds and plants to see what would grow best in American soil (he even smuggled into the country a particular variety of rice from Italy). As an architect, he designed and built Monticello, his home in Virginia, drew up plans for the Virginia state capital, and helped direct the building of the nation's capital at Washington, D.C.

Jefferson, however, is remembered mostly for his writings and his political philosophy. An extremely intelligent and well-read man, he believed the law could be used best as a powerful force to shape or change a society. He also believed in the people, the common laborers and farmers. If they were enlightened by education, Jefferson thought, they could better govern themselves instead of being governed by the ruling classes or the wealthy. His clearest statement of this belief is the Declaration of Independence.

Jefferson was born in 1743 at his father's plantation, "Shadwell," in central Virginia. As a child, he loved horseback riding and music, even learning to play the violin. But he was also very serious about his studies. By the age of nine, he already knew the basic elements of Latin, Greek, and French. Jefferson's love of books and learning continued throughout his life. His political beliefs as an adult also had their beginnings in his childhood, as he absorbed the democratic views of the farmers and the frontiersmen around him.

While at the College of William and Mary, Jefferson continued studying foreign and classical languages. He also became interested in mathematics and the natural sciences. But the greatest influence on his thinking came from William Small, Jefferson's mathematics and philosophy professor. Small introduced Jefferson to the ideas of the Enlightenment, a philosophic movement of that time. Jefferson's later political writings, especially the Declaration of Independence, would show the great influence this movement had on him.

After graduating from college in 1762, Jefferson studied law for five years under George Wythe, a famous Virginian lawyer. Jefferson soon thought he could help improve American society by entering politics. In 1769 he joined the Virginia House of Burgesses (the lower house of the colonial legislature), serving for six years. During this time, he became a leader in the movement opposing Britain's control over the American colonies. His essay *A Summary View of the Rights of British America,* written in 1774, described his views. Although many colonists thought Jefferson's arguments were too extreme, his ability as a writer was recognized. Two years later, as a member of the Second Continental Congress in Philadelphia, he

The Enlightenment

This philosophic movement of the eighteenth century suggested, based on scientific discoveries, that man's reason (intellect) could help him solve any problem. Since there were natural laws and uniform patterns in the universe, like gravity and the movement of planets, men believed there were natural laws behind everything, including political and social behavior. If these laws could be discovered and followed, people could live in harmony and society would naturally improve. The English philosopher John Locke believed all men had basic natural rights to life, liberty, and property. Governments, he believed, were organized to protect these rights. Other philosophers in this movement included the German Gottfried Wilhelm von Leibniz and the Frenchmen Voltaire and René Descartes.

was appointed to a committee to write the Declaration of Independence. Except for minor changes by other committee members, Jefferson wrote the document by himself. He completed the work in 18 days, without referring to books or notes.

During the American Revolution, Jefferson served as a member of the Virginia legislature and then as the governor of the colony. There he tried to turn his philosophical ideals into reality. He worked for religious freedom and against unfair practices concerning the inheritance of land and wealth. In 1783 Jefferson again served as a delegate to the Continental Congress, where he wrote rules for the governing of the Northwest Territory. Adopted a few years later as the Northwest Ordinance of 1787, these rules banned slavery in the territory north of the Ohio river and established how new states were to be admitted to the Union.

Clashes With Alexander Hamilton

In 1785 Jefferson succeeded Benjamin Franklin (see **Benjamin Franklin**) as minister to France, remaining in this position long enough to see the beginning of the French Revolution in 1789. He returned to the United States shortly afterward and was appointed by U.S. President George Washington (see **George Washington**) to be his secretary of state. A series of conflicts soon developed between Jefferson and Alexander Hamilton, the secretary of the treasury. Jefferson believed the federal government should be concerned mostly with foreign affairs. The states and local governments—led by farmers and workers—should handle local matters. Hamilton, on the other hand, believed in a strong central government under the control of wealthy merchants and property owners. Their debate caused two groups to form: backers of Hamilton became known as Federalists, while those who supported Jefferson became known as Republicans or Democratic Republicans (the modern Democratic Party traces its origin to this group).

The Washington administration adopted Hamilton's ideas, and in 1793 Jefferson resigned from the cabinet. He ran for the presidency three years later, narrowly losing to his friend John Adams. At that time, however, the second-place finisher became vice-president, so Jefferson accepted this position. But the Federalist Adams and the Republican Jefferson soon disagreed over many issues during Adams's administration. This was especially true with the passage of the Alien and Sedition Acts. These acts restricted the voting rights of recent immigrants and interfered with newspapers that criticized the government. Jefferson thought this seriously limited the freedoms of speech and of the press and, therefore, was contrary to the Constitution. Many people agreed with him.

Becomes Third President of U.S.

In the election of 1800, where American voters were given their first clear-cut choice between political parties, Jefferson defeated Adams. He eventually served two terms, during which he cut government spending and simplified the way government was run. But his major achievement was the Louisiana Purchase in 1803. It nearly doubled the size of the United States and cost less than three cents per acre. This vast area, rich in minerals and grazing land, allowed Americans to seriously begin their westward expansion.

Jefferson retired to Monticello in 1809, having been in politics almost continuously for 40 years. He turned his attention to architecture, farming, and education. In 1819, he designed and founded the University of Virginia, even selecting its faculty and planning its curriculum. Jefferson renewed his friendship with John Adams in 1813, and over the next 13 years they corresponded warmly. Both men died on July 4, 1826, 50 years after the signing of the Declaration of Independence.

Juana Inés de la Cruz

Mexican nun and poet

*Born in 1648,
San Miguel Nepantla, New Spain, present-day Mexico*

*Died April 17, 1695,
Mexico City, New Spain*

"Even though the pressures of her male-dominated society finally proved too much, her achievements had already been made."

Spain began conquering lands in the New World in 1519. By 1535 the Spanish king officially ruled the area from present-day Central America north to the southwestern United States. Known as "New Spain," this area remained a colony of the Spanish crown for nearly three hundred years. Early in this colonial period in Mexican history, society was almost unquestionably controlled by men. But one woman—Juana Inés de la Cruz—rose to question the unfair rank assigned to her and to other women. In a world where only men could receive an advanced education, she fought to become a poet and scholar on her own. Even though the pressures of her male-dominated society finally proved too much, her achievements had already been made. Today she is considered by many to be the finest lyric poet of Mexico's colonial period.

She was born Juana Inés Ramírez in 1648 in the village of San Miguel Neplanta. Her unmarried parents were Isabel Ramírez and Pedro Manuel de Asbaje y Vargas Machuca. She learned to read by the age of three and spent most of her time in her grandfather's library. When she was eight years old she went to Mexico City to live with her aunt. She continued studying on her own, learning Latin in only 20 lessons when she was nine. Since only men could attend the university, Juana dreamed of disguising herself as a man in order to enter. On one occasion she even cut her hair short.

By the time she was 16, Juana's intelligence and beauty had captured the interest of Marquesa Leonor de Mancera, the wife of the viceroy (governor) of New Spain. She appointed Juana as one of her ladies-in-waiting, and Juana charmed the viceroy's court with her wit and personality. But she gave up this privileged position at court two years later when she chose to become a nun. Given the options for women in Mexican society then, this was a wise choice. As a nun, she could manage her own property, acquire books for her own library, and spend a good part of her day reading and studying.

Broadens Her Studies as a Nun

On February 24, 1669, she entered the convent of San Jerónimo. Upon becoming a nun, women were asked to change their names as a reflection of their new religious lives. Henceforth, Juana became known as Sor (Sister) Juana Inés de la Cruz ("of the Cross"). Her life as a nun suited her. She took an active part in the politics of the convent and was elected three times to the post of bookkeeper. Managing her own finances, she increased her personal wealth, which allowed her to pursue her academic interests. She bought a number of scientific instruments and conducted many experiments in her cell at the convent. Surrounded by over 4,000 books in her library, Sor Juana painted and wrote poetry and plays. She also entertained many professors from the University of Mexico, discussing mathematics, astronomy, theology, and other matters.

Sor Juana eventually wrote three volumes of poetry and plays. Her first collection, *Inundacion castalida de la unica poetisa, musa decima,* was published in 1689. She wrote passionate sonnets and poems that combined her love of art and science in an almost mystical way. Her most famous poem, "El sueño" ("The Dream"), describes the soul as it flies in a dream toward knowledge. She also wrote poems that confronted the common sexist views in her society. To promote the idea of female wisdom and ability, she often referred to Greek and Egyptian mythological figures, such as the Egyptian goddess of nature, Isis. Other times she was not so subtle in her technique, as indicated in the title of one of her well-known poems, "Hombres necios" ("Stupid Men").

Although Sor Juana's poems attracted attention, they did not threaten her society. But when she openly challenged the male-controlled world of religion, many believed she had gone too far. In November 1690 she published a letter criticizing a sermon given by a Jesuit priest. This priest was the favorite of the archbishop of Mexico, a man Sor Juana disliked. By attacking the Jesuit, she also attacked the archbishop, and this proved to be her undoing.

Letter Defends Education of Women

The bishop of Puebla, using the false name of a nun, wrote a letter scolding Sor Juana for choosing nonreligious literature and philosophy over her religious studies. She responded to this attack with "Respuesta a Sor Filotea" in March 1691. In this now-famous letter she defended not only her broad education but the education of women in general. She argued that the study of the arts and sciences was the best way to know the natural world created by God. And she believed that since God had given her a keen intellect, it was her duty to use it as well as any man.

Although a few friends came to her defense, the majority of people now attacked Sor Juana for what they saw as arrogance on her part. Even the other nuns at San Jerónimo turned against her. Early in 1694, her morale and spirit finally broken, Sor Juana sold her vast library and all other possessions and retreated into convent life. When an epidemic swept through the convent the following year, she cared for many of the nuns who had previously turned their backs on her. As a result, she contracted the unknown disease and died on the morning of April 17, 1695. Today Juana Inés de la Cruz is recognized as one of the first feminists in the Americas and is honored with her portrait on Mexico's currency.

John F. Kennedy

Thirty-fifth president of the United States

Born May 29, 1917,
Brookline, Massachusetts

Died November 22, 1963,
Dallas, Texas

John F. Kennedy was president of the United States for just over a thousand days. Upon his election, he had called for domestic reforms through his New Frontier plan. He accomplished only a few of these goals as foreign crises arose to dominate his administration. Before he could fully tackle the issues that faced him at home, Kennedy was tragically assassinated. The mystery of his death and the possibilities of what he might have done create a legend that lasts to this day.

Kennedy was born in Brookline, Massachusetts, in 1917. He was the second of nine children born to Joseph and Rose Fitzgerald Kennedy. Because his father was one of the richest men in America, the young Kennedy grew up without having to suffer from the economic hardships of the Great Depression in the 1930s. Repeated illnesses during his youth, however, forced him to spend many hours alone reading in bed. Nonetheless, Kennedy was not a caring student until 1940, his senior year at Harvard University. Concerned about World War II, which had just begun in Europe, he wrote his senior

"The mystery of Kennedy's death and the possibilities of what he might have done create a legend that lasts to this day."

essay on why England was not prepared for war. Published as *Why England Slept,* it became a best-seller.

Rescues Fellow Sailors in South Pacific

When America entered the war in December 1941, Kennedy enlisted in the navy. He was given command of a PT boat, a small, fast craft used to torpedo large ships. On August 2, 1943, a Japanese destroyer rammed and sank Kennedy's PT-109 as it lay near the Solomon Islands in the southwest Pacific. Although his back was badly injured, Kennedy helped save the lives of several crew members. For his bravery, he received several medals.

After the war, urged on by his father, Kennedy ran for Congress. He campaigned hard and won convincingly in 1946. During his three terms as a Democrat in the House of Representatives, he worked tirelessly for public housing and other social programs for his district. In 1952 Kennedy decided to run for the United States Senate. Again, he was victorious. The following year, he married Jacqueline Lee Bouvier, the daughter of a wealthy Rhode Island family.

Kennedy underwent two dangerous, near-fatal operations on his ailing back in 1954. During his recovery, with assistance from a few aides, he wrote *Profiles in Courage.* This book, a study of American political leaders, was awarded the Pulitzer Prize for biography in 1957. At the 1956 Democratic Convention, Kennedy came close to winning the vice-presidential nomination. Elected to the Senate again in 1958, he rose through the Democratic party. At the 1960 convention, he won the presidential nomination on the first ballot.

During the campaign, Kennedy faced Republican challenger Richard Nixon in a series of live television debates, the first in history. In the November election, Kennedy won by a margin of only 12,000 votes out of the almost 70 million cast. He became the youngest person and the first Roman Catholic to have ever been elected president. In his eloquent and stirring inaugural speech, Kennedy outlined his New Frontier program. It included a tax cut, an increase in the space program, and action on the issue of civil rights. He also chal-

lenged Americans to "ask not what your country can do for you—ask what you can do for your country."

Foreign affairs quickly grabbed Kennedy's attention. The cold war, uneasy relations between communist and noncommunist governments, was at its height. As "Leader of the Free World," he felt it necessary to fight communism. He was particularly concerned about the communist government Fidel

Castro had recently created in Cuba. Kennedy backed a Central Intelligence Agency (CIA) plan to have anti-Castro Cubans invade the island and overthrow Castro. On April 17, 1961, the invasion took place at the Bay of Pigs but failed.

World Threatened by Nuclear War

During that summer, relations between Kennedy and Soviet Premier Nikita Khrushchev broke down. Communist forces in East Germany then built the Berlin Wall in August, preventing East Berliners from escaping to the West. One of the greatest threats to world peace took place just over a year later. In October 1962, American spy planes discovered nuclear missile sites in Cuba. Kennedy immediately ordered a naval blockade of the island so that no more weapons could reach it from the Soviet Union. He then demanded that Khrushchev remove the missiles. For a week, the world waited as the two men refused to back down. Finally, Khrushchev ended the Cuban missile crisis by agreeing to remove the missiles. In response, the United States withdrew its missiles from Turkey.

Kennedy faced another communist threat in Southeast Asia. The United States had signed a treaty in 1961 pledging to help South Vietnam in its fight with communist North Vietnam. At first, the United States sent only military aid and a few hundred military advisors. As the Vietnam War grew, however, Kennedy sent more of these advisors. Soon, he sent American troops to help in the fighting.

Not all of Kennedy's foreign affairs involved conflict. In 1961 he established the Alliance for Progress, which sent economic aid to Latin American countries. That same year he organized the Peace Corps. Still in existence today, this agency sends volunteers to help people in needy countries around the world. In addition to teaching languages and science, these volunteers offer training in areas such as farming and environmental conservation.

Some of Kennedy's accomplishments at home included assuring the admittance of African Americans into the Universities of Mississippi and Alabama. He also established a program to increase the hiring of African Americans in government agencies. Other major civil rights programs he called for did not come about during his presidency. For example, Congress did not act on the civil rights bill he introduced in June 1963 until after his death. Other principal reform measures Kennedy offered—a tax cut, federal aid for education, a program to fight poverty, medical care for the elderly—were either killed or not acted on by Congress.

On November 22, 1963, Kennedy traveled to Dallas, Texas, to give a speech. While riding through the streets in an open car, he was shot and killed. The police arrested Lee Harvey Oswald, a communist supporter, and charged him with the assassination. Before he could be tried, Oswald was murdered in a Dallas police station by Jack Ruby, a night-club owner. On November 25 Kennedy was buried in Arlington National Cemetery across the Potomac River from Washington, D.C.

The nation mourned Kennedy's death. The young president had brought a new outlook to the Oval Office. He had given many Americans, especially young people, renewed hope in what government could accomplish. Many people thought he was at the height of his political power and only needed more time to achieve his reforms. On November 29, President Lyndon Johnson appointed a commission to investigate the murder. The Warren Commission, headed by Supreme Court Chief Justice Earl Warren, concluded that Oswald had acted alone in the crime. To this day, however, many people believe Kennedy was killed as the result of a plot by several people or groups.

Martin Luther King, Jr.

Civil rights leader

*Born January 15, 1929,
Atlanta, Georgia*

*Died April 4, 1968,
Memphis, Tennessee*

*"More than any other
person, King guided
the anger of African
Americans into a
nonviolent movement
for social justice."*

In 1955 Martin Luther King, Jr., led African Americans to boycott the buses in Montgomery, Alabama. The boycott was only the beginning of the crusade to end the Southern system of segregation (the practice of separating blacks and whites, especially in public places). More than any other person, King directed the anger of African Americans into a nonviolent movement for social justice. His work helped bring down many of the barriers that separated African Americans from equality. He became a national symbol in the revolution for civil rights. Tragically, he was assassinated before his dream of a fair America became a reality.

King was born on January 15, 1929, in Atlanta, Georgia, where segregation was a way of life. Blacks and whites had separate schools, hospital waiting rooms, and even drinking fountains. When both were allowed into the same room, lines were drawn on the floor to keep them divided. King's parents, Martin Luther and Alberta King, taught him that he could overcome the humiliation of segregation. His father, who had grown up in poverty, rose to become a prominent Southern preacher.

Supported by his parents' teachings, King excelled at school, especially in public speaking. After completing high school early, King enrolled in Morehouse College in Atlanta in 1944. At this prestigious school for African American men, he majored in sociology and English and continued to participate in public speaking contests. He had planned to attend medical or law school, but professors at Morehouse urged him to become a minister.

Upon his graduation in 1948, King went to Crozer Theological Seminary in Pennsylvania to study religion. Here, he first learned of the activities of Mohandas Gandhi (see **Mohandas Gandhi**), who used nonviolent means (boycotts, protests) to help free India from English rule. Gandhi's teachings greatly inspired King. After earning his degree from Crozer in 1951, he began doctoral studies at Boston University in philosophy and religion. He was awarded his Ph.D. in 1955. While at the university, he met and married Coretta Scott.

Leads Montgomery Bus Boycott

In 1954 King accepted the position of pastor at the Dexter Avenue Baptist Church in Montgomery, Alabama. That same year, the Supreme Court ruled in *Brown v. Board of Education* that "separate but equal" schools for blacks and whites were unconstitutional. The racial climate in America soon changed as many African Americans began to challenge other segregation laws. The bus system in Montgomery operated under such a law: blacks and whites had separate seats. On December 1, 1955, seamstress Rosa Parks was arrested for refusing to give up her seat to a white man. In response, King and other African American leaders urged Montgomery's black community to boycott the city's buses on December 5.

After the boycott began successfully, King and the others formed the Montgomery Improvement Association to work for fairer laws. Chosen the group's president, King negotiated with city officials to change segregation in the bus system. They refused his demands and the boycott continued for 382

Martin Luther King, Jr. (second from left), with President John F. Kennedy.

days. Finally, on December 21, 1956, the Supreme Court ruled that the segregation of city buses was unconstitutional.

This victory convinced King and the others to spread the movement for civil rights across the South. In 1957 they organized the Southern Christian Leadership Conference. As the group's leader, King toured the country over the next few years giving speeches, attending rallies, and setting up protests. In

1963 King traveled to Birmingham, Alabama, to organize a protest against segregation in downtown department stores. At the time, this city was considered the most segregated in the nation. The Birmingham police moved against the protesters with clubs and attack dogs. King was arrested and placed in solitary confinement, where he wrote his famous "Letter from Birmingham Jail," eloquently arguing for the moral right of his movement. Because of the protestors' efforts, Birmingham's white businessmen agreed to halt their racial practices.

March on Washington

On August 28, 1963, over 200,000 people—black and white—marched on Washington, D.C. Organized by King, this rally sought to raise the nation's awareness about civil rights and to encourage Congress to pass the civil rights bill submitted by President Kennedy (**see John F. Kennedy**). At the end of the peaceful demonstration, King delivered his famous "I Have a Dream" speech.

For his leadership in the nonviolent fight for equality, King was awarded the Nobel Peace Prize in 1964, the youngest person ever to win the award. Earlier that year, King had witnessed the signing of the Civil Rights Act of 1964. It forbid racial discrimination in public places such as restaurants and theaters. Over the next year, King and others worked to end the use of poll taxes and literacy tests that prevented many African Americans from voting. In August 1965, Congress passed the Voting Rights Act of 1965, which legally ended those practices.

While continuing his work for civil rights, King widened his concern to include human rights. In 1967 he spoke out against the Vietnam War. Later that same year, he began a campaign to fight poverty in America. He toured the country to recruit people for a new march on Washington to demand

> ### From the "I Have a Dream" Speech
>
> "So I say to you today, my friends, that even though we must face the difficulties of today and tomorrow, I still have a dream. It is a dream deeply rooted in the American dream that one day this nation will rise up and live out the true meaning of its creed—we hold these truths to be self-evident, that all men are created equal."

economic rights for everyone. During this tour, he went to Memphis, Tennessee, to speak on behalf of striking sanitation workers. On April 4, 1968, while standing on the balcony of the Lorraine Motel in Memphis, King was shot and killed by James Earl Ray.

Mother Ann Lee

Founder of the Shakers

*Born February 29, 1736,
Manchester, England*

*Died September 8, 1784,
Niskeyuna, New York*

The Shakers remain both a mystery and an attraction for many Americans today. In 1840 over 6,000 members belonged to this religious sect and lived in communities from New York to Kentucky. Their true name was the United Society of Believers in Christ's Second Coming, but they were better known as Shakers for their wild dancing during times of worship. They were founded in America by their spiritual leader, Ann Lee, whom they called "Mother Ann." Her aphorisms, or guiding principles, directed the Shakers to live simply and to work toward perfection in everything they did. Lee was a pioneer for justice and peace, and the Shakers became the first group in America to practice true democracy, treating men and women of all races equally.

Lee was born in 1736 in the working-class slums of Manchester, England. Her father, John Lee, was a blacksmith whose meager income barely fed his family of eight children. Lee received no education and she never learned to read or write. From a young age she worked fourteen-hour days in the cotton

"Lee was a pioneer for justice and peace, and the Shakers became the first group in America to practice true democracy, treating men and women of all races equally."

mills of Manchester. She escaped the mills by the time she was twenty, only to work as a cook in a public insane asylum. The filth and crowdedness of the city offended Lee, and she became especially sickened by drunkenness and sexual promiscuity.

In 1758, seeking spiritual relief, Lee joined a religious group led by former Quakers James and Jane Wardley. Quakers believed they could find spiritual truth in their own hearts and did not need priests and organized rituals. The Wardleys were also influenced by the Camisards, a group of French prophets who believed in the second coming of Jesus Christ (see **Jesus of Nazareth**). During their religious meetings, Camisards often shouted in different languages and shook violently. The Wardleys adopted these practices and their group became known as the "Shaking Quakers" or "Shakers."

Four years after Lee met the Wardleys, her father forced her to marry his apprentice, Abraham Standerin. Over the next several years, she gave birth to four children, all of whom died very young. Feeling she had been punished by God for not being celibate, Lee decided to remain so for the rest of her life. She then devoted herself completely to the Shakers. Their loud and frenzied worship and their practice of disturbing other religious services angered their neighbors. Shakers were beaten and arrested on many occasions. During one of these imprisonments, Lee supposedly received a vision that the Shakers came to regard as the birth of their movement.

Has Vision of Christ

In 1772, while in a small cell, Lee reportedly had a vision of Jesus Christ who told her she was his successor. The Shakers accepted Lee's vision and made her their new leader, calling her Mother Ann. Fleeing the continued violence they faced in England, she and eight followers (including her brother, William Lee) sailed to America in 1774. They worked in New York City while searching for a place to build their own community. They found it in the deep, swampy wilderness of Niskeyuna, New York, and in September 1776 Lee founded the first Shaker community there.

Niskeyuna benefitted from a religious revival called the Great Awakening that had swept through America in the middle of the century. Settlers on the frontier lands had a hard life, and they sought comfort in the teachings of traveling preachers. When the Shakers created their community, many people gladly accepted the Shakers' way of life.

Lee directed her followers to live by her 11 aphorisms, such as "Let your words be few, and seasoned with grace" and "Be faithful with your hands, that you may have something to give to the poor." Work was especially important to the Shakers. They treated all of their daily activities as a form of worship, whether building a house, planting a garden, or making a chair. Today, people are still drawn to the perfection of a Shaker building and the simplicity of a Shaker chair.

Lee established strict rules in the area of reproduction—sexual relations, even between spouses, was strictly forbidden. Therefore, men and women lived in different quarters. Under Lee's guidance, however, everyone was treated equally—men, women, black, white. The Shakers often bought slaves, gave them freedom, and accepted them into their community to work and to worship freely.

The Shakers' unusual form of worship—dancing, singing, shaking—frightened many people. Mobs gathered outside of Shaker services to shout insults or to throw stones at them. The Shakers' belief in pacifism (opposing war and violence) during this time of the American Revolution proved to be an even greater danger. Because Shaker leaders were English and did not believe in the war, they were considered Tories (English supporters). In the summer of 1780, Lee was accused of treason and put in prison for five months before the governor of New York pardoned her.

Beaten While Trying to Preach

Despite these events, interest in the Shakers increased. In May 1781, Lee, her brother, William, and a few other Shakers

---

Shaker Hymn

'Tis a gift to be simple, 'tis a gift to be free

'Tis a gift to come down where we ought to be,

And when we find ourselves in the place just right,

We'll be in the valley of love and delight.

When true simplicity is gained,

To bow and to bend we'll not be ashamed,

To turn, turn, will be our delight,

Till by turning, turning, we come round right.

---

set out on horseback to gather new converts in Connecticut, Maine, and Massachusetts. Their preaching mission lasted more than two years and they established several new communities throughout New England. Despite the success of their mission, however, they faced repeated acts of mob violence. Several Shakers were horsewhipped; others were tied and dragged behind horses. Lee herself was pulled from a house, beaten, and thrown into a carriage. Among her many injuries, Lee had suffered a fractured skull. By the time the party returned to Niskeyuna in the autumn of 1783, both Lee and her brother had been fatally injured. She died on September 8, 1784, less than two months after her brother.

Supported by Lee's teachings, the Shakers continued to grow, reaching their height in 1840 with 18 communities. Without new converts, however, they were doomed by their vow of celibacy. By 1925 only six communities remained. In the early 1960s the few remaining Shakers decided not to accept any new members. Mother Ann Lee and Shakerism, though, had left a lasting mark on American culture.

Robert E. Lee

Confederate general during the American Civil War

Born January 19, 1807, Stratford, Virginia

Died October 12, 1870, Lexington, Virginia

Robert E. Lee's ancestors played a vital role in the creation and early development of the United States. Two of his father's cousins, Richard Henry Lee and Francis Lightfoot Lee, were among the 56 signers of the Declaration of Independence. His father, Henry "Light-Horse Harry" Lee, was a war hero who fought under General George Washington during the American Revolution. After the war, he served in Congress and as a three-term governor of Virginia. Lee's mother, Ann Hill Carter, came from a respected family that had long held prominent positions in Virginia's government and society. Still other members of Lee's extended family were part of Virginia's upper class.

Although Lee was born into this aristocracy in 1807, he never enjoyed its accompanying wealth. His father wasted the family's fortune in a series of bad investments. After serving a year in a debtor's prison in 1809, Henry Lee left his family for the West Indies. Thus, from early boyhood, Lee was left to care for his mother who had become an invalid. Perhaps

"Lee thought slavery was a 'moral evil' and secession was 'unconstitutional,' but he believed his first duty was to his home state of Virginia."

because of these hardships, he grew up with a heightened sense of duty and honor. The values his mother taught him of "self-denial and self-control" marked him for the rest of his life.

After his formal education in Alexandria, Lee entered the United States Military Academy at West Point in 1825. Academically, he was always near the top of his class. Militarily, he was the top of his class. In four years he did not receive a single demerit (penalty), and his fellow cadets called him the "Marble Model." Because of his excellent record, he was commissioned into the army's famed Corps of Engineers after his graduation in 1829. Two years later, he married Mary Anne Randolph Custis, a great-granddaughter of Martha Washington, and settled in her family's home in Arlington, Virginia.

Lee first achieved military distinction in the Mexican War. Beginning in 1846, the United States and Mexico fought over land claims in the southwest region of the United States, particularly over Texas. Serving under army commander Winfield Scott, Lee made several scouting trips that led to the capture of Mexico City. Wounded in battle, he showed extreme bravery and was promoted from captain to colonel by the war's end in 1848. Four years later, he received the distinguished assignment of superintendent of West Point. He held this post for three years before the War Department transferred him to a cavalry regiment in southwest Texas.

Captures John Brown at Harpers Ferry

The growing issue over slavery in the United States soon involved Lee. In October 1859, the fiery abolitionist John Brown and his antislavery followers seized a government arsenal at Harpers Ferry, Virginia. Lee was ordered to lead a company of marines against this rebellion. After Brown refused to surrender, Lee's forces assaulted the building and in three minutes defeated Brown's tiny band. This violent episode outraged Southerners, who believed the North was trying to do away with their way of life. The southern desire to secede (break away) from the Union reached its peak when Abraham Lincoln (see **Abraham Lincoln**) was elected president in

November 1860. The following February, the Confederate States of America was formed, and two months later the Civil War began.

Lee thought slavery was a 'moral evil' and secession was 'unconstitutional,' but he believed his first duty was to his home state of Virginia. He refused command of the Union forces and resigned from the army on April 20, 1861, two days after Virginia seceded. Lee assumed command of Virginia's military and naval forces and accepted the position of general in the Confederate army. His was given the initial task of protecting western Virginia against Union attacks, but failed. Still having faith in Lee's abilities, Confederate President Jefferson Davis placed him in charge of the defenses of the South Atlantic coastline in November. Lee responded well to this new assignment.

Davis recalled Lee to the Confederate capital of Richmond, Virginia, on March 2, 1862. Under the command of General George B. McClellan, a new Union army—the Army of the Potomac—planned to attack Richmond. As Davis's military advisor, Lee worked to coordinate the defenses of the capital city. He ordered General Thomas J. "Stonewall" Jackson to take the offensive in the nearby Shenandoah Valley. This campaign worked: reinforcements to the Union army were cut off. McClellan remained a threat, however, when Confederate commanding general Joseph E. Johnston was wounded at the battle of Fair Oaks near Richmond in May. Davis then turned the Army of Northern Virginia over to Lee.

Once in command, Lee immediately ended McClellan's threat in what came to be known as the Seven Days' battles (June 26-July 2). After withdrawing from Richmond, McClellan tried to transfer his men to the army of Major General John Pope. Before they had time to combine their forces, Lee attacked Pope at the second battle of Bull Run in Virginia on August 29-30. The Northerners were routed. To threaten Washington, Lee then marched his men into Maryland. McClellan learned of Lee's plans and met him at Antietam on September 17. The ensuing battle was a draw, but the Union army had succeeded in stopping the Confederate invasion.

Fails at Battle of Gettysburg

Lee spent the next eight months blocking any Union advance on Richmond. In December 1862, the Confederates brutally defeated the Union forces at the battle of Fredericksburg in Virginia. The following May, the Union army lost again, this time at the battle of Chancellorsville in Virginia. This victory cost the Confederates 10,000 soldiers, including General Jackson, who was accidentally shot by one of his men. After this, Lee took the offensive once again and moved into Pennsylvania. This drive north ended when the Confederates accidently met Union forces at Gettysburg on July 1. Even though both sides suffered heavy losses during this three-day battle, the Confederates were defeated. Lee blamed the loss on himself and offered Jefferson Davis his resignation. The Confederate president refused it.

Lee did not take part in any major campaigns until he met Union General Ulysses S. Grant (see **Ulysses S. Grant**) the following year at Petersburg, Virginia, just south of Richmond. From June 1864 to April 1865, Grant assaulted the city and the surrounding area, but Lee's defenses held. Losses soon mounted on both sides. While Grant could replenish his army with men and supplies, Lee could not. Eventually, the Confederate lines were too weak to hold off the Union forces. On April 2, 1865, they gave way, and Richmond had to be abandoned. Not wishing to see his men suffer any more, Lee surrendered to Grant at Appomattox Courthouse on April 9.

When the Civil War ended, Lee encouraged Southerners to work toward peace and unity. After returning to Richmond, he accepted the presidency of Washington College (now Washington and Lee University) in Lexington, Virginia. He earned admirers in both the North and the South with his quiet dignity. He swore renewed allegiance to the United States, but Congress refused to restore his citizenship. Lee died on October 12, 1870, after suffering a heart attack.

Abraham Lincoln

Sixteenth president of the United States

Born February 12, 1809,
Hardin County, Kentucky

Died April 15, 1865,
Washington, D.C.

In the southern states of America, it was referred to as the War between the States. In the northern states, it was officially called the War of the Rebellion. In modern times it is known as the Civil War, the bloodiest conflict in America's history. Many stories have been written about its battles and the people who fought them. Of these stories, many have changed into myths. It is often difficult to find the truth in the myths surrounding the lives of famous people in history. Abraham Lincoln's life is such an instance.

Lincoln was born in a log cabin in the backwoods of Kentucky in 1809. His parents, Thomas Lincoln and Nancy Hanks, were poor, illiterate farmers. As a boy, Lincoln was closer to his mother than to his father. When she died in 1819 after the family had moved to Indiana, he turned to his older sister Sarah for guidance. Since his father thought he would become a farmer, Lincoln received less than a year of formal schooling. He did educate himself, though, by reading over and over the few books he could obtain.

"Although Lincoln believed he would be remembered most for signing the Emancipation Proclamation, he is remembered more for his speech dedicating a national cemetery in 1863 at Gettysburg, Pennsylvania—the Gettysburg Address."

After his sister's death in 1828, Lincoln had little reason to stay with his father. He joined a flatboat expedition down the Mississippi River. This four-month voyage gave him his first glimpse of parts of the country he hardly knew existed. In 1831, after his family had resettled in Illinois, he volunteered for that state's militia to fight Native Americans in what became known as the Black Hawk War. Although he never saw any battles, he was elected captain by his company. He left the militia in 1832, settled in New Salem, Illinois, and worked at a variety of jobs, including general store owner, town postmaster, and surveyor.

In 1834, as a member of the Whig party, Lincoln was elected to the Illinois state legislature, serving until 1841. During his first term, he taught himself law and earned his license to practice in 1836. He moved to Springfield the following year and began traveling throughout the state trying court cases. On November 4, 1842, he married Mary Todd, and over the next eleven years they had four sons: Robert, Edward, William, and Thomas.

Lincoln was elected to the U.S. House of Representatives in 1847, but he accomplished very little and served only one term. Disappointed, he returned to Springfield, vowing to stay out of politics. The growing issue of slavery in America, however, soon pulled him back. In 1820 Congress had passed the Missouri Compromise, which permitted Missouri to be admitted as a slave state while banning slavery in the remaining northern portions of the Louisiana Purchase. This compromise, though, was nullified when Congress passed the Kansas-Nebraska Act in 1854. Sponsored by Illinois Senator Stephen A. Douglas, this act allowed the settlers of those two new territories to decide whether slavery would be permitted. Angered over the possible spread of slavery, Lincoln ran for his state's other Senate seat in 1855, and lost.

Gains Notice for Debates with Douglas

A group of people who opposed the Kansas-Nebraska Act formed the Republican party in 1854. Identifying with the ideas of this party, Lincoln joined in 1856 and quickly became

a leader. When Douglas, a member of the Democratic party, ran for re-election as state senator in 1858, the Republicans nominated Lincoln to run against him. The two men then met for a series of seven debates across the state. Their fiery discussions over the issue of slavery expansion drew large crowds and national press coverage. The election in 1859 was close, but Douglas won and returned to Washington.

President Abraham Lincoln visits soldiers at Antietam, Maryland, on October 3, 1862.

Lincoln's performance in the debates, however, earned him the Republican nomination for president in May 1860. Lincoln received only a minority of the popular vote, but won the November election by receiving a majority of the electoral college vote. Panic swept through the South. Many extremists, believing Lincoln would do away with slavery after he was inaugurated, urged the Southern states to secede (break away) from the Union. South Carolina became the first state to do so on December 20. Mississippi, Florida, Alabama, Georgia, Louisiana, and Texas soon followed suit. On February 4, 1861, these states formed the Confederate States of America, drew up a new constitution, and elected Jefferson Davis their president. Lincoln had not yet set foot in the White House.

After his inauguration in March 1861, Lincoln sought to hold onto all federal property in Confederate territory. He sent ships to resupply the federal military post at Fort Sumter in South Carolina. At dawn on April 12, the Confederates fired on the ships and the fort, starting the Civil War. Lincoln and the North were unprepared to meet this rebellion. Tens of thousands of untrained men volunteered to serve, but the Union army lacked everything from shoes to muskets to supply them. Several high-ranking Union officers defected to the Confederacy. Under poor leadership, the Union army had to retreat from the first major skirmish of the war, the first battle of Bull Run in Virginia on July 21. (Confederates called it the first battle of Manassas.)

Lincoln was criticized during the initial stages of the war. The Union army fared poorly, and Lincoln could not find a general to properly lead it. Members of Lincoln's cabinet ignored him and tried to make their own decisions and policy. Many people thought he acted like a dictator when he limited the freedom of the press and allowed the army to arrest suspected traitors without proof. Lincoln believed these actions were necessary, though, to achieve his main goal—keeping the United States together. His secondary goal, ending slavery, was not shared by most Northerners, therefore, he could not push for it while the war went poorly. In September 1862, however, after the Union forces stopped the Confederates from moving north at the battle of Antietam in Maryland, Lincoln began work on this goal. On January 1, 1863, he signed the Emancipation Proclamation, which declared all slaves in the Confederate states permanently free.

Delivers Famous Gettysburg Address

Although Lincoln believed he would be remembered most for signing the Emancipation Proclamation, he is remembered more for his speech dedicating a national cemetery in 1863 at Gettysburg, Pennsylvania—the Gettysburg Address.

He was not the main speaker and many people at the time felt his short speech—just 272 words—was dull and did nothing to honor the occasion. People later realized that, through his clear and vivid language, he honored not only the dead but the very ideals on which the United States was founded.

Lincoln finally found a capable general in Ulysses S. Grant (see **Ulysses S. Grant**) and gave him command of the Union forces in March 1864. Lincoln, though, truly remained the commander in chief, overseeing all aspects of the war. To educate himself in military history and strategy, he borrowed books from the Library of Congress. Through it all, Lincoln had to battle his critics. While some Northerners accused him of putting too much emphasis on the issue of slavery, others thought he was not putting enough. Many people just wanted an end to the war. It was not guaranteed, then, that Lincoln would be re-elected at the end of 1864. Even Lincoln, himself, thought his chances were not very good.

From the *Gettysburg Address*

Four score and seven years ago our fathers brought forth on this continent a new nation, conceived in Liberty, and dedicated to the proposition that all men are created equal.

Now we are engaged in a great civil war, testing whether that nation or any nation so conceived and so dedicated, can long endure. We are met on a great battlefield of that war. We have come to dedicate a portion of that field, as a final resting place for those who here gave their lives that that nation might live. It is altogether fitting and proper that we should do this,

But, in a larger sense, we can not dedicate—we can not consecrate—we can not hallow—this ground. The brave men. living and dead, who struggled here, have consecrated it, far above our poor power to add or detract. The world will little note, nor long remember what we say here, but it can never forget what they did here. It is for us the living, rather, to be dedicated here to the unfinished work which they who fought here have thus far so nobly advanced. It is rather for us to be here dedicated to the great task remaining before us—that from these honored dead we take increased devotion to that cause for which they gave the last full measure of devotion—that we here highly resolve that these dead shall not have died in vain—that this nation, under God, shall have a new birth of freedom—and that government of the people, by the people, for the people, shall not perish from the earth.

However, the fall of Atlanta to Union General William Tecumseh Sherman on September 2 helped boost Northern hopes that the war would end soon. Lincoln won the November election.

Afterward, Lincoln lobbied Congress to adopt the Thirteenth Amendment, which would ban slavery throughout the United States. It passed on January 31, 1865. For the next few months, Lincoln worked hard on a peace plan to end the war. Even though the Confederacy refused his offers, he remained hopeful. On April 9, at Appomattox Courthouse in central Virginia, Confederate General Robert E. Lee (see **Robert E. Lee**) surrendered his troops to General Grant. The Civil War was over.

Lincoln had been sworn in for his second term as president just a month before, but how he would have handled the rebuilding of the divided nation can only be imagined. On April 14, while watching a play at Ford's Theater in Washington, he was shot by John Wilkes Booth, an actor who sided with the South. Lincoln was carried to a boardinghouse across the street. He died early the next morning, becoming the first U.S. president to be assassinated. Secretary of War Edwin M. Stanton, who had been standing by the bed, reportedly said to the others gathered there, "Now he belongs to the ages."

Malcolm X

African American revolutionary

Born May 19, 1925,
Omaha, Nebraska

Died February 21, 1965,
New York City

Malcom X's political philosophy has long been associated with violence. In his fight for equality and justice for African Americans, he called for violence as an important means of self-defense. At one time in his career Malcolm X believed that blacks and whites could never be united in America. His views, however, changed — he came to favor not only African American freedom but the unity of all oppressed people throughout the world.

He was born Malcolm Little in Omaha, Nebraska, on May 19, 1925. The seventh child of Earl, a Baptist minister, and Louise Little, Malcolm grew up in a world of racism and poverty. Early in his childhood, the Ku Klux Klan (a white racist group), attacked his home, shattering all the windows. After moving to Michigan, his family was attacked again by another racist group known as the Black Legion, who burned his family's house to the ground. In 1931 his father was killed, perhaps by this same group.

"Malcolm X came to favor not only African American freedom but the unity of all oppressed people throughout the world."

The early 1930s was the worst period of the Great Depression in America. Malcolm's family sank deeper into poverty. His mother, upset over her family's condition and the loss of her husband, became mentally ill and was confined to a state mental hospital. The family was broken up in 1937, and over the next few years Malcolm lived with several foster families. After completing the eighth grade, he moved to Boston in 1941 to live with his aunt. He never went back to school.

During the next five years, Malcolm fell into the world of crime. Known as "Detroit Red" (because of his reddish complexion and hair), he sold illegal liquor and drugs and committed armed robberies. In 1946 he was caught while trying to have a stolen watch repaired and was sentenced to ten years in jail.

Prison marked a turning point in Malcolm's life. Other inmates introduced him to the ideas of Elijah Muhammad and the Black Muslims—followers of the religion of Islam. This religious group held the beliefs that black people were racially superior, that white people were devils, and that it was necessary for blacks to separate themselves totally from whites. Like traditional Muslims, this group emphasized cleanliness and forbade smoking, drinking, and the eating of pork. Encouraged to resume his education, Malcolm read all the books he could find in the prison library. He even copied the dictionary word by word.

Becomes Malcolm X

Upon his release from prison in 1952, Malcolm joined the Black Muslims and became known as Malcolm X (all members took "X" to represent the name of their forgotten African tribe). He quickly grew into an intelligent and energetic speaker. Within two years, he helped found temples in Boston and Philadelphia. Because of Malcolm's exceptional abilities, Muhammad appointed him minister of the New York City temple, one of the most important in the country. In 1958 Malcolm married fellow Black Muslim Betty X, and over the next six years they had four daughters.

In the late 1950s, the national news media began to focus on the growing Black Muslims. Although Malcolm always referred to himself as Muhammad's representative, his fiery speeches against white oppression made him the Muslims' leading spokesman. The media tried to spotlight the idea that Malcolm called for racial violence. In response, Malcolm explained that he merely encouraged African Americans to defend themselves against racial violence, not cause it.

Malcolm's growing popularity disturbed some leaders in the Black Muslims because they thought he was becoming too powerful. For his part, Malcolm began to disagree with the Muslims' practice of staying out of politics. Seeing the partial gains of the civil rights movement in the South, he thought political action might be necessary for African Americans to achieve justice. After Muhammad learned of Malcolm's growing beliefs, he began to move against his disciple.

When President John F. Kennedy (see **John F. Kennedy**) was assassinated in November 1963, Malcolm referred to the shooting as "the chickens coming home to roost." Many people believed Malcolm was saying the president deserved to be shot. He explained later that he meant the country's hatred had killed the president. Either way, Muhammad seized this chance to suspend Malcolm from the Black Muslims for 90 days.

Malcolm soon learned, however, that members of the Black Muslims were possibly planning to assassinate him. Convinced he could not remain with the group, he left on March 8, 1964, and founded Muslim Mosque, Inc. He declared that, unlike the Black Muslims, his new movement would take an active part in the civil rights campaigns of the South. Then on April 13, he left the United States to make a "hajj."

Pilgrimage Changes View About Races

A hajj is a pilgrimage (journey) to the holy city of Mecca, Saudi Arabia, the birthplace of the Islamic Prophet Muhammad (see **Muhammad**). Every Muslim is expected to take this pilgrimage at least once. Malcolm became known as El-Hajj Malik El-Shabazz after he was accepted into the traditional Islamic religion. While traveling to Mecca, Malcolm saw something he had never seen in America: people of all races united in their beliefs. This experience altered his previous view that all whites were racists and that blacks and whites had to remain separate.

On his way back to America, Malcolm visited many African countries and had private meetings with several African heads of state. He came away from these sessions with a deeper sympathy for oppressed people around the world. He still believed in black nationalism, the idea that African Americans had to gain control of their own communities and organizations before they could gain their freedom. To help achieve this, Malcolm formed the nonreligious Organization of Afro-American Unity upon his return to America.

As an independent leader in the fight for African American rights, Malcolm received death threats from numerous groups—notably the Black Muslims and white racists. On February 14, 1965, his home was firebombed. Though he and his family escaped unharmed, the house was destroyed. One week later, Malcolm gave a speech at the Audubon Ballroom in Harlem, New York. Included in the audience were his pregnant wife and four daughters. A few minutes into the speech, three men rose and fired sixteen shots into Malcolm. Two of the three men arrested for his assassination were members of the Black Muslims. Although there are theories of other groups being involved in the murder plot, no evidence has ever been produced.

Thurgood Marshall

Supreme Court justice, lawyer

*Born July 2, 1908,
Baltimore, Maryland*

*Died January 24, 1993,
Bethesda, Maryland*

"He brought us the Constitution as a document like Moses brought his people the Ten Commandments." This statement by an official of the National Association for the Advancement of Colored People (NAACP) clearly describes the life of Thurgood Marshall. Although he was the first African American to serve on the United States Supreme Court, Marshall should be remembered best as the greatest civil rights lawyer of his time. During the 1940s and 1950s, he won almost every civil rights case he argued before the Supreme Court. He fought against what he saw as injustice. In doing so, he helped change the lives of all African Americans.

There is very little in Marshall's childhood to show that he would grow up to be a great lawyer. He was born on July 2, 1908, in Baltimore, Maryland. His parents named him "Thoroughgood" after his grandfather who had fought for the Union during the Civil War. But Marshall shortened his name to "Thurgood" when he started school. Since both his parents

"He never gave up his fight for racial equality and the victims of injustice."

worked, his mother as a teacher and his father at a variety of jobs, Marshall grew up comfortably in a middle-class neighborhood.

Marshall performed poorly in school, though. His grades were below average and he misbehaved in class. As punishment, his high school principal often made Marshall sit and read the Constitution of the United States. It was his first contact with the law. After high school, even with poor grades, Marshall attended Lincoln University. He hoped to become a dentist. But he did not improve his study habits in college. He failed a class and was expelled twice.

Marriage Changes Life

In 1929 Marshall's life was turned around. He met and married Vivian Burey, nicknamed "Buster," a student at the University of Pennsylvania. Burey gave Marshall the confidence and the discipline he needed to do well in school. He returned to Lincoln and graduated with honors in June of 1930. In the fall of that year, Marshall went to law school at Howard University in Washington, D.C. Howard was a major center for black scholars then, and Marshall studied with the best teachers. Three years later he graduated at the top of his class.

In 1933 Marshall returned to Baltimore and opened up his own law office. But white clients at that time would not go to a black lawyer, and Marshall struggled. By the fall of 1934, the NAACP had begun a legal battle to attack racial segregation (the belief that people of different races should be separated). Marshall offered at once to help the organization. Within a few months, he had won his first major civil rights case. In *Murray v. Pearson* (1935), Marshall argued before a Maryland court that the University of Maryland Law School could not prevent a black student from enrolling. The court agreed. Over the next few years, Marshall became known as a lawyer who studied carefully for his cases and who argued them with common sense.

In 1936 Marshall joined the NAACP's legal office in New York. Two years later, he was named the organization's chief counsel, or top lawyer. He was thirty years old. In his new position, Marshall had to travel around the country arguing cases before courts. This was especially dangerous in the South. There Marshall's life was threatened many times because he tried to end discrimination, or the idea that people should be judged differently, often because of their race or sex. He did not win every case he argued. But of the 32 cases he argued for the NAACP before the Supreme Court, he won 29.

Fights for Equal Education

The NAACP's main goal was to end racial segregation in public schools. In 1896 the Supreme Court had decided in *Plessy v. Ferguson* that "separate but equal" public schools for blacks and whites was constitutional, or legal under the Constitution of the United States. Separate schools were set up for blacks and for whites, but they were rarely equal. Black children often received a poorer education, especially in the South. Marshall and the NAACP fought against this inequality. In the early 1950s, Marshall won a number of cases that ended racial discrimination in colleges and universities. But his greatest victory came in 1954. The Supreme Court ruled in *Brown v. Board of Education* that separate public schools were harmful to black children, as Marshall argued, and that this was against the law under the Constitution.

After John F. Kennedy (see **John F. Kennedy**) was elected president in 1960, he selected Marshall to serve as a judge on the U.S. Court of Appeals for the Second Circuit, an important court just below the Supreme Court. Marshall held this post until 1965. President Lyndon Johnson then named him solicitor general. As solicitor general, Marshall was the assistant to the attorney general, the chief lawyer for the federal government. He was the first African American to be placed in this position. Two years later, President Johnson nominated Marshall to become a justice on the U.S. Supreme Court. Marshall served honorably on the high court for almost 24 years, finally retiring on June 27, 1991, at the age of 82. Although his achievements as a judge and justice never equaled his earlier ones as a lawyer, Marshall remained faithful to his ideals. He never gave up his fight for racial equality and the victims of injustice.

José Martí

Cuban writer and revolutionary

*Born January 28, 1853,
Havana, Cuba*

*Died May 19, 1895,
Dos Ríos, Cuba*

"Banished from Cuba for his political views, the young Martí used his writings to rally support for his people."

Spain began its conquest of Cuba in 1511. After having destroyed the several different native tribes living there, the Spanish replaced them with African slaves. The island then became a base from which the Spanish explored and conquered other areas in the Americas. These areas eventually gained their independence at the beginning of the 1800s, but Cuba remained under Spanish rule. A ten-year revolt on the island, beginning in 1868, brought about some governmental reforms but not complete independence. It took the gifted writer and patriot José Martí to lead the final revolutionary struggle. Banished from Cuba for his political views, the young Martí used his writings to rally support for his people. Although his death came early in the battle for independence, his spirit spurred his fellow Cuban revolutionaries to victory.

Martí was born into a poor family in the Cuban capital of Havana in 1853. After having excelled in his primary schools, Martí was admitted to the respected Institute of Havana. Here, he became a disciple of the poet and teacher Rafael María de

Mendive. A strong Cuban nationalist, Mendive secretly worked for his country's independence from Spain. His political views greatly influenced the young Martí.

Between the years 1862 and 1867, Spain allowed Cuban intellectuals to express their views freely, and Mendive led the calls for reform. However, this openness came to an end when conservative forces took over the Spanish government in 1867. A brutal struggle for Cuban independence, known as the Ten Years' War, erupted the following year. Mendive was arrested. In response, Martí helped write and publish the newspaper *La Patria Libre* (*The Free Nation*). Authorities considered it rebellious and arrested Martí, who was only 16. He served six months of hard labor.

Banished to Spain after his release, Martí furthered his education. In 1874 he graduated from the University of Zaragosa with degrees in law and literature. He continued writing essays and poems and kept in touch with the ongoing revolution in Cuba. In 1875 he went to Mexico and contributed political articles to various newspapers. Two years later, he traveled to Guatemala, where he became a professor of literature in the Central School. The other writers there thought so highly of Martí that they elected him vice president of the national literary society. While in Guatemala, Martí met and married María Garcia Granados.

Returns to Cuba

The Treaty of Zanjón ended the Ten Years' War in 1878, and Martí returned to Havana with his wife. The authorities still considered him a threat and refused to let him teach or practice law. Because the government had not delivered on its promised reforms, a small group of people clung to the idea of independence. Martí was among them. He openly criticized the Spanish government and Cubans who did not support the movement. In September 1879, because of his political views, Martí again was arrested and exiled to Spain.

This time, Martí only remained in Spain for two months. In January 1880 he settled in New York City, home to a large community of exiled Cubans. Martí supported himself by giving speeches on Cuba and its independence movement. He also wrote political pamphlets and contributed poems and literary criticism to local newspapers such as the New York *Sun*. He traveled to Venezuela in 1881 and wrote articles for the prestigious newspaper *Revista Venezolana*. But his radical views upset Venezuela's dictator, Antonio Guzmán Blanco, and after just five months he was forced to return to New York.

Martí began writing regular columns for *La Opinión Nacional* of Caracas and *La Nación* of Buenos Aires, Argentina. His articles for these newspapers made him famous throughout the Americas. With his experiences in Mexico, Guatemala, and Venezuela, he no longer considered himself just a Cuban. He identified with all Spanish-speaking people in the Americas and urged them to support any country seeking independence from Spain. He admired the United States for its freedoms and educational opportunities, but detested the racism he saw in the country. Also, he feared that the powerful United States would try to take over Cuba after Spain granted it independence.

Writes New Style of Poetry and Fiction

During the 1880s, Martí traveled throughout the United States with hopes of raising support for Cuba's independence. In addition to his political writings, Martí wrote critical essays on such American writers as the essayist Ralph Waldo Emerson and the poet Walt Whitman. In 1885 he published *Amistad funesta* (*Ill-Omened Friendship*). Many literary critics consider this work to be the first modern-style novel written in Spanish. Martí's poetry also broke new ground. Although he felt poetry was sacred, he believed it was ultimately worthless unless it could be understood by all people. Therefore, he wrote in a clear and simple poetic style. In 1891 he published his best-known collection of poems, *Versos sencillos* (*Simple Verses*), featuring the themes of love and friendship.

Even though he became famous for his literary writings, Martí remained devoted to the independence cause. In the early 1890s he founded the Cuban Revolutionary party and planned for a new war of independence. As leader of the movement, he officially called for Cubans to rise up against Spain on January 29, 1895. Along with General Máximo Gómez and other rebels, Martí sailed to the island of Santo Domingo and then to Cuba. They landed on the southeast coast on April 11. Fourteen days later, the rebels met a large Spanish force on the plains of Dos Ríos in the present-day province of Santiago de Cuba. Grabbing a pistol, Martí ran into the middle of the vicious battle, where he was shot and killed by a Spanish rifleman. After Martí's death, more revolutionaries rose up on the island, and by 1898 the Spanish had been driven from Cuba.

Increase Mather

Puritan clergyman and writer

Born June 21, 1639,
Dorchester, Massachusetts

Died August 23, 1723,
Boston, Massachusetts

"As a minister, writer, educator, and politician, Mather was perhaps the greatest spokesperson for the ideals of Puritanism in America."

Puritanism was a religious movement that arose in England during the mid-sixteenth century. Puritans were members of the Church of England who objected to the political structure of the Church and to its continued use of Roman Catholic rituals in the services. Some Puritans, called Separatists, wanted simply to break with the Church of England and organize their own churches according to their beliefs. Because Separatists were severely persecuted in England, a great many of these Puritans migrated to the Massachusetts colonies in America during the 1630s. By 1640 more than 20,000 of them had sailed over the Atlantic.

The Puritans tried to create a "godly society" where their ideals of independence and hard work governed all aspects of life. Eventually, they were successful. Puritanism became an important force both in the religion and in the politics of the New England colonies. It also gave America its first writers, and one family—the Mathers—came to dominate Puritan intellectual life for three generations. Increase Mather was the first member of this family to be born in America and was its most gifted. As a minister, writer, educator, and politician, he was perhaps the greatest spokesperson for the ideals of Puritanism in America.

Mather was born in Massachusetts in 1639, six years after his parents, Katherine and Richard Mather, took part in the great Puritan migration. In addition to regular schooling, Mather was taught Greek and Latin by his father, the minister of a Puritan church in Dorchester, Massachusetts. He completed his bachelor's degree at Harvard College in 1656 and sailed the following year to Ireland to attend Trinity College in Dublin. After graduating with a master's degree in 1658, Mather preached at various Puritan churches around England.

Restoration Forces Mather From England

A civil war in England in the 1640s had resulted in the beheading of King Charles I in 1649. The monarchy was removed and a democratic form of government, called the Commonwealth, was set up. The Commonwealth soon collapsed, however, and in 1660 the monarchy was restored with Charles II on the throne. This period in history is known as the Reformation. Charles II insisted that everyone obey the guidelines of the Church of England, so Puritans like Mather again fled the country. Within a year after his return to Massachusetts, Mather married Maria Cotton, daughter of the prominent Boston minister John Cotton. In 1663 she gave birth to the beginning of the third generation of Mathers, a son named Cotton.

Mather became minister of the Second Congregational Church in Boston in 1664. For the next 20 years he sharpened his preaching skills and wrote over 25 books, among them a biography of his father, *The Life and Death of Richard Mather,* and a report of the battles with the local Native Americans, *A Relation of the Troubles in New England by Reason of the Indians.*

Mather had kept in close contact with Harvard College and in 1685 he was elected its president. Harvard had been established in 1636 to educate Puritan ministers, but Mather worked to broaden its curriculum. He had a deep interest in the sciences. In 1684 he wrote *Essay for the Recording of Illustrious Providences,* a scientific investigation of strange natural happenings. That same year he founded the Boston Philosophic Society, the first scientific academy in New England.

In 1684 Mather turned his attention away from religion and academics to politics. English king Charles II canceled the charter of the Massachusetts Bay Colony and placed a new governor in control of the area. Mather led the protest against this new governor and English control. In 1688 he journeyed to England hoping to obtain a new charter from the new English monarchs, William and Mary. His negotiations were successful and in 1691 a new charter was granted. It united the Massachusetts Bay Colony with Plymouth Colony to its south, and returned most of the governmental control of this area to the colonists. The king, however, kept the right to appoint the governor of Massachusetts.

Criticizes Salem Witch Trials

When Mather returned from England in 1692, the infamous Salem witch trials were under way. Though he believed in the existence of witches and evil spirits, Mather did not believe in the justice of the trials. Almost all of the evidence against those accused was based on rumor, and Mather feared that many innocent people might be wrongly convicted. His fears were not shared by those in power and 20 people, mostly women, were eventually convicted and hanged. Mather condemned the trials and the verdicts in his *Causes of Conscience Concerning Evil Spirits.*

Over the next 10 years Mather's popularity declined. The new charter and the new governor both were unpopular, and the people of Massachusetts blamed Mather. His position in society was threatened mostly, though, because of his conservative ideals. More liberal views were starting to spread through the colonies, and Mather was forced to resign the presidency of Harvard in 1701 because he would not soften his strict religious beliefs.

After this, Mather stayed out of public affairs, focusing on his preaching and writing. But when a smallpox epidemic swept through Boston in 1721, bringing fear and death, Mather and his son Cotton came forward. Because of their interest in science and medicine, they were aware of the new medical treatment called inoculation. In this procedure a small amount of a disease is put into a body so that defenses can then be built up against it. While Mather and most of his fellow ministers supported a smallpox inoculation, most of Boston's doctors opposed the idea. In the end, more of those who were inoculated survived than did those who were not.

Mather died in the arms of his son Cotton on August 23, 1723. In his lifetime he had written over 150 books, mostly on religious matters. Cotton shared his father's conservative views and love of writing, publishing some 450 books. But he died only five years after his father, bringing the great line of Puritan intellectuals to an end. Even though the severe religious aspects of Puritanism soon faded, its ideals of independence and hard work remained to become a part of the American tradition.

Moctezuma II

Aztec emperor

*Born c. 1480,
Tenochtitlán, present-day Mexico City, Mexico*

*Died June 30, 1520,
Tenochtitlán*

"The Aztec were at the cultural height of their civilization during the reign of Moctezuma II."

I n 1492 Christopher Columbus accidentally discovered what Europeans came to call the New World. It was new, though, only to them. Many native tribes of people already lived throughout the continents of North and South America. In present-day Mexico City there existed a people known as the Aztec. They founded their glorious capital city, Tenochtitlán, around 1325, and over the next two centuries this city grew and its people prospered. During the reign of Moctezuma II, who became emperor in 1502, the Aztec were at the cultural height of their civilization. This was also the time when Spanish conquistadors (conquerors) began exploring and claiming lands in the New World for their king, Charles V (see **Charles V**). The riches of the Aztec lured the conquistador Hernán Cortés, and he destroyed their empire just 30 years after Columbus's landing.

The ancient capital of Tenochtitlán was beautiful. *Chinampas* (floating gardens) dotted the waters of the surrounding Lake Texcoco. The massive *teocallis* (temples) and wide plazas of the city shone white in the sun. The clean, orderly streets overflowed with trees, flowers, and vegetable gardens. The air was filled with their aroma and with the songs of birds. Throughout Tenochtitlán the Aztec had built and tended aviaries— shelters where birds could nest. Thousands of them filled these aviaries.

The Aztec loved poetry and music, and they created a written language and an incredibly accurate calendar. They were very advanced in architecture, astronomy, engineering, and mathematics. They were also very religious, and they worshipped hundreds of gods. In the Aztec world, these gods controlled everything, and the only purpose of living was to serve them. This was done through elaborate ceremonies, which included animal and human sacrifices.

Aztec Offer Sacrifices to Gods

Religion and war dominated Aztec society. Their chief god was Huitzilopochtli, the god of war. The Aztec continually battled surrounding tribes, mostly to capture enemy warriors to sacrifice to Huitzilopochtli and the other gods. A prisoner would be led to the top of the high temples where a priest would cut out his heart, lift it into the sunlight, then toss it into a dish. The Aztec believed the spilled blood provided the gods with their needed *chalchiuatl* ("precious water"). Portions of the victim's body were used in stews to feed the Aztec and the skull was added to one of the massive *tzompantli* (skull racks) in the square.

Moctezuma, the sixth son of Emperor Axayácatl, was born around 1480. Like other royal children, he learned to be both a warrior and a priest. He became a successful fighter and a high-ranking priest, and in 1502 he was chosen to become the *Uei Tlatoani* ("the one who speaks"). As emperor, Moctezuma led his people both as a military and a spiritual leader. In the early years of his reign, he conquered lands and tribes as far away as present-day Nicaragua. In 1509, however, he gave up battle and devoted himself to the worship of the gods.

Aztec religion foretold that in 1519 the fair-skinned god of morning, Quetzalcóatl, would return from the east and take

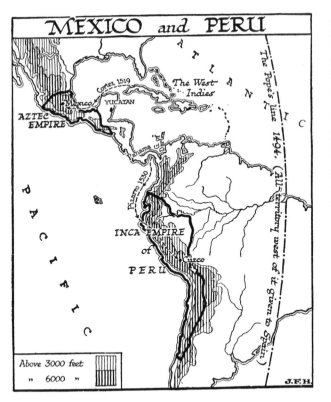

MEXICO and PERU

AZTEC EMPIRE

Cortez, 1519

Mexico
YUCATAN

The West Indies

The Pope's line 1494. (All territory west of it given to Spain.)

Pizarro 1530

INCA EMPIRE of PERU

Cuzco

PACIFIC

Above 3000 feet
"   6000   "

J.F.H.

over the Aztec world. In October of 1519 Moctezuma's spies reported that fair-skinned men had arrived on the coast from the ocean. Moctezuma and the Aztec believed these men were descendents of Quetzalcóatl. In reality, they were the Spanish, led by Hernán Cortés. After quickly learning of the rich Aztec society from surrounding tribes (some of them enemies of the Aztec), Cortés and his men set out for Tenochtitlán. When they entered the city on November 8, 1519, they were welcomed as honored guests and given feasts and gifts. Allowed free run of the city, the Spaniards were amazed by the beauty, the cool air, and the fragrant smell of Tenochtitlán.

Moctezuma Held Captive

Seven days after arriving, Cortés took Moctezuma prisoner, hoping to control the Aztec through their emperor. Cortés wanted their riches, but as a devout Catholic he also wanted to put an end to their religion with its human sacrifices. He humiliated Moctezuma, even placing him in chains at one point. Because the emperor did not rebel, his people grew angry with him. Moctezuma finally decided to turn against the Spaniards when, the following spring, Cortés smashed the face of the statue of Huitzilopochtli.

On May 16, 1520, while Cortés and many of his men were away from the city, the remaining Spaniards attacked the Aztec during one of their religious celebrations. Hundreds were killed and the Aztec rose in revolt, demanding Moctemuza's release. The rebellion continued until Cortés returned on June 24. He refused to let the emperor go free, and the Aztec declared war on the Spaniards. They fought with a fury, and Cortés and his men were trapped in the palace. Cortés brought out Moctezuma to speak to his people, but the palace remained under attack and Moctezuma was accidentally shot by arrows. He died three days later. The enraged Aztec then drove the Spaniards out of the city.

The following year Cortés returned, and for 90 days he and his army attacked Tenochtitlán. On August 13, 1521, the city fell and the Aztec empire came to an end. Nothing of beauty remained as Cortés had even burned the aviaries to the ground. In addition to Christianity and horses, the Spanish conquistadors also brought diseases like smallpox to the New World. Within 50 years of their arrival, 90 percent of the native peoples of present-day Mexico were dead.

Thomas Paine

Political philosopher and writer

Born January 29, 1737,
Thetford, Norfolk, England

Died June 8, 1809,
New York City

"While many people helped the cause of the American Revolution by using a gun, Paine helped by using a pen."

As a writer, Thomas Paine's thoughts were rarely original: he mostly used ideas that already existed. What made him special was the way he combined those ideas and presented them in a language best understood by the common man. His writings were forceful and persuasive. He sailed to America from England just before the fight for independence began and became involved immediately. While many people helped the cause of the American Revolution by using a gun, Paine helped by using a pen. He defended liberty not only for the people in America but also for those in England and in France. In his humanitarian support for social welfare policies, he was a man ahead of his time.

Paine was born in Thetford, England, on January 29, 1737. After seven years of school, he apprenticed to his father, a corsetmaker. Young Paine had little interest in the business, though, and ran away to sea at the age of 16. He soon returned, finished his apprenticeship, and worked in several towns before owning his own shop. In 1759 he married Mary Lambert. When she died suddenly the following year, Paine abandoned his trade to become an exciseman (collector of taxes on goods produced and sold in a country). He remarried in 1768 and continued his education by reading books, attending lectures, and conducting scientific experiments.

Paine entered the world of politics in 1772 by writing a pamphlet calling for pay increases for excisemen. The new salaries were denied and Paine was fired from his job. He went bankrupt and was divorced from his second wife, but his career of fighting for reform had begun. His work caught the attention of Benjamin Franklin (see **Benjamin Franklin**), who was in London pushing for American independence. Franklin encouraged Paine to sail to America and gave him a letter of recommendation. Armed with this letter, Paine traveled to Philadelphia in 1774 and found work with the new *Pennsylvania Magazine.*

Pamphlet Raises Support for Revolution

While writing for the magazine, Paine drew in the revolutionary spirit growing around him. In January 1776, he presented arguments for America's independence from England in his pamphlet *Common Sense.* Written in clear, everyday language, it rallied all the colonists to the cause of the American Revolution. Because of the pamphlet's popularity, 25 editions had to be published during that year.

Paine then enlisted in the Continental army and served as a military aide, but he continued to raise support for the American war effort through his writings. In December 1776 he began publishing *The Crisis,* a set of 16 inspiring essays, the first of which began with the now-famous line "These are the times that try men's souls." It was read to the men commanded by General George Washington (see **George Washington**) after they crossed the Delaware River and surprised the English army at Trenton, New Jersey.

A few years after the war ended and America gained independence, Paine sailed back to England to work on the design of an iron bridge. With the outbreak of the French Revolution in 1789, however, he was drawn back into political conflict. Many people criticized the Revolution for trying to overthrow the monarchy. Paine, on the other hand, supported it and responded to this criticism in 1791 by writing a two-part work, *The Rights of Man.* Like other great people of his time, Paine was influenced by the Enlightenment. This philosophical movement held that natural laws (civil rights) existed for all people, and governments were only formed to protect them. Paine argued that if people were fighting for a truly representative government, then their fight was just. He further argued that it was the duty of governments to provide universal education, unemployment relief, and assistance for the poor.

Because he criticized the English monarchy in this work, Paine was threatened with imprisonment for treason. In 1792 he fled to France where he was welcomed as a hero and was elected to the National Convention, the country's new body of representatives. Paine, however, soon opposed the mob violence of the French Revolution and the execution of French king Louis XVI. Branded a traitor, he was jailed from December of 1793 to November of 1794.

Attacks Christianity

During this time, Paine wrote *The Age of Reason,* in which he attempted to define his belief in the religious philosophy called Deism. Deists did not reject God, but thought God set up the universe like an intricate clock and left it running, never to interfere with it. They believed the Bible was only a moral guide, and that the natural laws of the universe (and God's perfection) could be discovered through education and reason. Paine urged people to abandon Christianity, which he called "absurd" and "contradictory," and to follow a natural religion of good deeds and humanitarianism.

This work proved to be Paine's undoing. Upon his return to America in 1802, he faced great hostility. Many people saw *The Age of Reason* as an attack on society and labeled him an atheist (a person who does not believe in God). Even those people who had supported his earlier writings turned against him. His great accomplishments as a champion of liberty soon faded from their memories. Paine, who had argued on behalf of the poor throughout his life, lived his last seven years in poverty. He died alone in New York on June 8, 1809.

Juan Domingo Perón

Politician, president

*Born October 8, 1895,
Lobos, Argentina*

*Died July 1, 1974,
Buenos Aires, Argentina*

Eva Marie Duarte de Perón

Political leader and confidant

*Born May 7, 1919,
Los Toldos, Argentina*

*Died July 26, 1952,
Buenos Aires, Argentina*

I t is hard to separate the reality from the myth in Juan and Eva Perón's lives. He led one of the most important revolutions in Latin America in the twentieth century. And together, Juan and Eva helped the poor and working class of Argentina more than anyone. Although there are some who claim the Peróns became too powerful and controlled too much, while they ruled, they captured the hearts and minds of their supporters. It is Perón's idea of social justice, glorious for a time, that has stayed with many Argentines to this day.

"The names of Juan and Evita Perón still have a magical meaning for many Argentines."

**Juan Domingo Perón
Eva Marie Duarte de Perón**

The rest of the world has come to know their lives through the hit Broadway musical *Evita*.

Juan Domingo Perón was born in 1895 in the small town of Lobos in the Buenos Aires province of Argentina. While he was growing up, his life was very unsettled. Perón's family moved often to search for better living conditions. By the time he was nine, he had to leave his family completely to go to school in Buenos Aires. Having to fend for himself, he grew up quickly. But he was a poor student, and when he was 15 he decided against going to college. Instead, he entered the Colegio Militar, the army's military academy. Here, with the other boys, he felt the closeness of family that he had never enjoyed as a child. He graduated in 1913 as a second lieutenant in the infantry, and was promoted to lieutenant two years later. By 1919, he began to show signs of being a leader.

That same year, when Perón was 24, Eva Duarte was born outside the village of Los Toldos in the Buenos Aires province. Her mother, Juana Ibarguren, was unmarried. Her father, Juan Duarte, was a respected landowner married to the sister of the mayor of Chivilcoy, a neighboring town. He died suddenly in 1926. When Juana took Eva and her four other children—all fathered by Duarte—to his funeral, a fight broke out between Eva's family and her father's other, legitimate, family. Faced with this scandal, Eva's family had to move to a larger city when she was 12. Three years later, Eva left home for the glamour of Buenos Aires.

In the meantime, Perón's standing in the army began to rise. Promoted to captain in 1924, he was assigned only two years later to the Escuela Superior de Guerra (Superior War College). After training there for the next three years, he graduated and then married Aurelia Tizon. His life seemed to be going well. By 1931, he was selected to serve on the faculty of the War College for five years. Here he developed the writing and speaking skills that would later help him as a politician. But in 1938, his wife died from cancer, and his world almost fell apart. He gained control of his life shortly afterward, however, when he was sent to train troops in Italy.

Eva's star did not rise as quickly as Perón's. In Buenos Aires, she tried desperately to become an actress, but could

Juan and Eva Perón

get only very small roles in second-rate plays and movies. After a few years, she tried for parts on radio soap operas and was successful. By 1943, Eva was a recognized soap-opera star with her own company. Soon she would come to Juan Perón's attention.

Perón had returned to Buenos Aires in 1942 as a full colonel, but he found the military and the government divided. Some leaders wanted Argentina to enter World War II, while others wanted the country to remain neutral, or stay out of the war. It was during this period of unrest that Perón created a secret military society, the G.O.U., or *Grupo de Oficiales Unidos* (Group of United Officers). Many people felt the government was becoming dishonest, and on June 4, 1943, the G.O.U. staged a military coup, or takeover of the government.

Perón Moves Into Politics

Perón was determined to have political power. Under the new military government, he became the undersecretary of

Juan Domingo Perón
Eva Marie Duarte de Perón

war and the secretary of labor. He did away with government policies that hurt workers, giving them better working conditions and higher salaries. He understood their problems and tried to solve most of them. Workers across Argentina began to support Perón. It was at this time, in January 1944, that Perón first met Eva, or as she was better known, Evita. She became his mistress, which caused a small scandal. Some people wondered if Perón should be seen with an "actress," an occupation not held in high regard at that time. Perón did not care. He was becoming powerful.

In October 1945, Perón's hold on power began to slip. The military, tired of running the government, decided to hold elections. Fearful that Perón would run for president and become too powerful, the military had him jailed. Workers from across Argentina supported Perón, however, and on October 17 hundreds of thousands of them jammed the Plaza de Mayo, a city square, and demanded Perón's release. Perón was freed, becoming even more popular. Four days later, he married Evita, and the following February, he won the presidency.

In his first term as president, Perón brought the country together. He believed in social justice and economic independence. He increased the wages of workers, gave aid to the poor, and helped Argentina pay off its foreign debt, or money it owed to other countries. Evita aided her husband's efforts by creating the Eva Perón Foundation, which gave money and gifts to the poor. Workers soon began carrying banners praising the Peróns.

To some, however, the Peróns were becoming too strong. Perón had started his own political party, the Peronist Party, over which he had total control. He also removed from government those who did not agree with him. And in 1951, during the next election, Perón tried to have Evita run as his vice presidential candidate. Leaders in the military blocked this. It was a defeat for Perón. But he suffered even more when Evita died from cancer the following year. Many believed Perón changed after her death. His new policies, like legalizing prostitution and divorce, began to disturb more people. Argentina's economy declined. Finally, in 1955, Perón was forced by the military to give up the presidency, and he fled to Spain.

The new government tried to remove Perón's and Evita's names from streets, documents, and places. It even forbid the Peronist Party from taking part in the political process. But the Peróns were remembered by the workers they had helped. In 1973 the government was forced to allow the Peronist Party to enter the presidential election. Although they won, the new president was not qualified and had to resign later that year. Perón, who had maintained control over his party from Spain, entered the new elections and won. He was old, though, and running the unstable Argentina proved too much for him. He died of a heart attack in July 1974. But the names of Juan and Evita Perón still have a magical meaning for many Argentines, and the Peronist Party has continued to play a major part in Argentine politics.

Juan Domingo Perón
Eva Marie Duarte de Perón

Eleanor Roosevelt

*Humanitarian and
First Lady of the United States*

*Born October 11, 1884,
New York City*

*Died November 7, 1962,
New York City*

"Through her humanitarian efforts in America and abroad, Roosevelt became one of the best-known and most admired women in the world."

Eleanor Roosevelt's extended family was among the ruling class in America in the first half of the twentieth century. Her uncle, Theodore Roosevelt, and her husband and fifth cousin, Franklin D. Roosevelt (see **Franklin D. Roosevelt**), both became presidents. Their accomplishments, however, did little to overshadow hers. While her husband was president, she helped develop or strongly supported many of the programs in his New Deal plan to rescue the country from the throes of the Great Depression. After his death, she continued working for the rights of the poor and the oppressed, this time on a global scale. Through her humanitarian efforts in America and abroad, Roosevelt became one of the best-known and most admired women in the world.

Anna Eleanor Roosevelt was born in New York City in 1884. She was the daughter of Elliot Roosevelt, brother of future president Theodore Roosevelt, and Anna Ludlow Hall. Her father, although loving, was an alcoholic; her mother was cold and disapproving. By the time she was eight, both of her parents had died, so she went to live with her grandmother. Awkward and shy, she was sent to finishing school in England when she was 15. Here the withdrawn Roosevelt blossomed, excelling in languages and literature and becoming popular for the first time in her life.

When she returned to New York City at age 17, Roosevelt refused to take part in the activities of high society. Instead, she chose to work toward social reforms. She taught dancing and literature at community centers and visited needy children in the slums. Through her work, she gained an intimate knowledge of how the poor actually lived. During this time, she met her fifth cousin Franklin D. Roosevelt. Against his mother's wishes, they were married on March 17, 1905. Her uncle, President Theodore Roosevelt, gave her away at the wedding. Over the next ten years, she gave birth to six children (one died in infancy).

Neither her family nor her husband's growing political career prevented Roosevelt from pursuing her own social concerns. While he served in Washington as assistant secretary of the navy during World War I, she worked with the Red Cross. She visited wounded troops in the Naval Hospital and worked to improve conditions at a hospital for the mentally ill. After Roosevelt and her husband returned to New York in 1920, she became active in movements calling for equal rights for women and better working conditions for female employees.

In the summer of 1921, Roosevelt's life changed drastically. While vacationing on an island off the coast of Maine, her husband was stricken with an attack of poliomyelitis (polio). The disease left him permanently paralyzed from the waist down. Determined to maintain her husband's political links, she quickly learned public speaking and political organization. Over the next few years, she campaigned for Democratic candidates in New York and worked for the women's division of the party.

Changes Role of First Lady

In 1928 Roosevelt's husband was elected governor of New York. She then became his "legs," inspecting state hospi-

The first telecast of Eleanor Roosevelt's weekly forum on February 11, 1950.

tals, prisons, and homes for the elderly. In 1932 he was elected to the first of four presidential terms, giving her a national platform from which to address her concerns. Roosevelt forever changed the role of the First Lady. She began holding weekly press conferences, speaking only to women reporters mainly on women's issues. In 1935 she started writing a column, "My Day," which appeared in national newspapers. For its first three years, "My Day" focused on the concerns of women. By 1939, however, Roosevelt was addressing general political topics in her column.

This change reflected the increasing role Roosevelt played in her husband's policy decisions. More than anyone in the White House, she brought the cause of the oppressed to her husband's attention. She championed the struggle of Appalachian farmers to reclaim their land, and she made sure African Americans were receiving relief from New Deal programs. Throughout her reign as First Lady, she argued against all forms of discrimination. Roosevelt was especially concerned with the condition of America's youth during the Depression. In 1935 she helped found the National Youth Administration, which gave thousands of high school and college students part-time work.

Roosevelt had always been a pacifist (person opposed to war and conflict), but supported the war effort when America entered World War II in 1941. She concentrated her energies on the welfare of American soldiers. In the summer of 1943, she traveled 23,000 miles visiting field hospitals in Australia and the South Pacific.

Champions Human Rights Around the World

After her husband died suddenly on April 12, 1945, Roosevelt continued her public activities. In December of that year, President Harry S. Truman appointed her a United States delegate to the first meeting of the United Nations in London. She became the chairperson of the Commission on Human Rights, which was given the job of drafting an international bill of rights. On December 10, 1948, the United Nations accepted the Universal Declaration of Human Rights. Roosevelt had been the driving force behind its creation.

When Republican Dwight D. Eisenhower became president in 1952, Roosevelt resigned her position at the United Nations. She became a leading spokesperson for liberal causes, arguing for civil rights not only in American but in all other

---

From the Universal Declaration of Human Rights

Article I

All human beings are born free and equal in dignity and rights. They are endowed with reason and conscience and should act towards one another in a spirit of brotherhood.

countries. Traveling around the world throughout the 1950s, she called for nuclear disarmament and urged leaders to protect the human rights of their people. Even in her late seventies, Roosevelt remained a powerful voice in the Democratic party. She died at her home in New York City on November 7, 1962.

Franklin D. Roosevelt

Thirty-second president of the United States

*Born January 30, 1882,
Hyde Park, New York*

*Died April 12, 1945,
Warm Springs, Georgia*

When he was just a child, Franklin D. Roosevelt had the opportunity to travel to the White House to meet President Grover Cleveland. At their meeting, Cleveland told the young boy never to become president. He did not listen. Roosevelt grew up not only to become president but to be elected four times. His administration lasted 12 years and 40 days, longer than any other president in American history. He guided the nation through two of its most dangerous crises—the Great Depression and World War II. Although Roosevelt's legislative program, known as the New Deal, ended in 1938, its results continue to affect millions of Americans to the present day. His plans offered relief, recovery, and reform. Even more, he gave America courage and hope during its darkest periods.

Roosevelt was born in 1882 in New York into a respected and wealthy family. He was the only son of James and Sara Roosevelt, and received most of his education at home from his mother. In 1900 he went to Harvard University where he

"Although Roosevelt's legislative program, known as the New Deal, ended in 1938, its results continue to affect millions of Americans to the present day."

majored in history and political science and wrote for the school newspaper. He graduated in three years. During his time at Harvard, Roosevelt met and courted his distant cousin Eleanor Roosevelt (see Eleanor Roosevelt). They were married on March 17, 1905. Eleanor's uncle, President Theodore Roosevelt, gave her away at the ceremony.

Roosevelt then entered law school at Columbia University. After just two years of study, he passed the New York bar exam and joined a respectable law firm. He began his political career in 1910 when he was elected as a Democrat to the New York State Senate. Even though he was only a freshman senator, he took an active role in the affairs of his political party. In 1912 he worked hard for the presidential nomination of fellow Democrat Woodrow Wilson. When Wilson won the election, he rewarded Roosevelt by naming him assistant secretary of the navy. After serving in this position for eight years, he resigned to run as the Democratic party's candidate for vice president. The Republicans, under Warren G. Harding, won easily, and Roosevelt returned to his law practice.

Struck Down by Polio

In August 1921, while vacationing on an island off the coast of Maine, Roosevelt was stricken with an attack of poliomyelitis (polio). The disease left him paralyzed from the waist down. He never regained full use of his legs and was confined to a wheelchair most of the time. Painfully, he worked to overcome his disability and learned to walk, at times, with leg braces and a cane or crutches. By 1928 he had made such a recovery that the leader of the Democratic party asked him to run for governor of New York. The election was close, but Roosevelt won.

On October 24, 1929, the stock market crashed. That day, the prices of stocks began to fall and people began to sell whatever stocks they owned. The more they sold, the more the prices fell. People's fortunes, tied up in the stock market, were wiped out. Businesses and factories soon closed, and people were laid off. Within a few years, almost one-third of American workers were unemployed. The Great Depression had begun.

One of Franklin Delano Roosevelt's live-radio broadcasts to the nation (1939).

Re-elected governor in 1930, Roosevelt had to face the effects of the Depression. He felt it was the duty of the state to care for those who could not care for themselves. He established reforms such as unemployment relief and pensions for the elderly. Under his leadership, New York became the first state to provide assistance to those in need. As a result, Roosevelt became the leading Democratic choice for president in 1932. At the Democratic National Convention in Chicago, he promised "a new deal for the American people." In November he soundly defeated Republican president Herbert Hoover.

New Deal Rescues Depressed Nation

Immediately after his inauguration on March 4, 1933, Roosevelt put his New Deal program into action. His first move was to gain power over the nation's banks and money system. He then flooded Congress with legislation to provide relief and reform for American workers. On March 31 Congress created the Civilian Conservation Corps (CCC). It put young men to work on public lands, fighting soil erosion and building dams, roads, and parks. On May 12 Congress formed the Agricultural Adjustment Administration (AAA). By paying farmers to plant only a certain amount of crops, the AAA ensured that farm prices would remain high and farmers could make a living.

Other acts passed by Congress provided grants to states and cities, regulated the stock market, and refunded farm mortgages. One of the most important bills of the New Deal program, however, was the National Industrial Recovery Act. It helped devise codes for industry, such as the prices of products, the maximum number of work hours, and the minimum pay for employees. It also guaranteed workers the right to organize unions and to bargain for wages.

Relief for the unemployed was Roosevelt's primary aim. In 1935 he set up the Works Progress Administration (WPA). It put unemployed people to work building and improving bridges, parks, hospitals, roads, and schools. Writers wrote reports or guidebooks of the states, while artists painted murals in post offices and other public buildings. The WPA and the CCC literally restored the lives of millions of people. After putting people back to work, Roosevelt focused on reform. Another important piece of legislation was the Social Security Act, which Congress passed on August 14, 1935. It provided retirement payments for workers plus benefits for widows, orphans, and the needy.

The World Turns to War

Because of his New Deal reforms, Roosevelt carried 48 states in the 1936 election. But within two years he was forced to shift his emphasis from domestic policy to foreign affairs as the threat of war grew in Europe. The stock market crash had affected the economies of many European countries. Seeking relief, millions of unemployed Germans turned to the extreme nationalist platform of Adolf Hitler (see Adolf Hitler) and the Nazi party. After coming to power in 1933, Hitler rebuilt the German economy by preparing to take over Europe. On September 1, 1939, he invaded Poland and started World War II.

Roosevelt understood the dangers Hitler posed to the free world, but Congress and most Americans did not want to get involved in the war. After winning his third election in 1940, Roosevelt did what he could to help Europe fight Hitler. In March 1941 he pushed the Lend-Lease Act through Congress. This allowed Roosevelt to give supplies to any country whose defense he deemed vital to America. In August of that year, he met with English Prime Minister Winston Churchill (see **Winston Churchill**) to discuss English-American relations and the possibility of creating a United Nations organization. Meanwhile, American relations with Japan worsened over trade disputes and Japanese aggression in China. On December 7, 1941, Japan attacked the American naval base at Pearl Harbor, Hawaii. America was now in the war.

Roosevelt skillfully managed the American war effort, making sure industries produced the necessary supplies for American soldiers. He also had several wartime conferences with Churchill and Soviet dictator Joseph Stalin. Together the three leaders plotted strategy against Hitler and his allies. Throughout the war, Roosevelt kept his dream of a United Nations alive. He won his fourth term as president in 1944, but his health was failing. While vacationing in Warm Springs, Georgia, on April 12, 1945, he suffered a massive cerebral hemorrhage and died. The war was not yet over, but Roosevelt had paved the way for American victory. The United Nations did not yet exist, but he had laid the groundwork for its creation.

José de San Martín

Argentine national hero

Born February 25, 1778,
Yapeyú, Argentina

Died August 17, 1850,
Boulogne-sur-Mer, France

"These were momentous times in South American history, and San Martín's military victories secured his place among the great fighters for independence."

For the first 22 years of his career, José de San Martín served in the Spanish army. He fought in North Africa, France, Spain, and Portugal during and after the French Revolution. Taken prisoner three times during battles, he was eventually promoted to the rank of lieutenant colonel for his bravery and skill. But when South America began to seek its independence from Spain in the early 1800s, San Martín changed his allegiance. He was a creole, a person of Spanish descent born in the New World, and he returned to his home country—present-day Argentina—to lead its fight. These were momentous times in South American history, and San Martín's military victories secured his place among the great fighters for independence.

San Martín was the youngest son of Juan de San Martín, a Spanish aristocrat, and Gregoria Mattoras. Born in 1778 in the town of Yapeyú in present-day Argentina, he moved with his family to Spain when he was seven. He went to the Seminario de los Nobles in Madrid, a school for the sons of military officers and of nobility. Although he did not do poorly, he showed no real talent in any subject. In 1798, at the young age of 11, he became a cadet in the Spanish army at Murcia, a province in southeast Spain. The French Revolution had begun less than a week before.

San Martín fought his first battle at the age of 13 in North Africa. His entire regiment was captured while trying to protect the Spanish-held port of Oran in present-day northwest Algeria. He returned to Spain after his release and took part in an invasion of France in 1793. Again, he was captured and this time, held for two years. Afterward, he participated in a naval campaign against England. In 1798 he was captured and held prisoner for a third time. Upon his final release, he fought in battles against Portugal (an ally of England) and against France when Napoleon (see **Napoleon I Bonaparte**) invaded Spain in 1808.

Leaves Spanish Army for Revolution

The brewing revolution against Spanish rule in his home country soon captured San Martín's attention. After having served Spain for over 20 years, he left to begin his fight against it. When he arrived in his homeland in 1812, he was named commander of the army. He wanted to liberate not only Argentina but all of South America. The Spanish, he believed, could only be defeated by removing them from their stronghold in Peru. To do that, he would first seal the independence of neighboring Chile.

From his years of military service in Spain, San Martín had learned the value of careful planning. He spent the next few years rebuilding his poorly trained army and plotting his attack on Peru. To raise support for his army, he took over the governorship of the present-day province of Mendoza in western Argentina. While secretly training his troops, he improved social and economic conditions in the province. Under his direction, farm production was expanded, irrigation canals were dug, and roads were improved. To stop the spread of smallpox, he had both civilians and soldiers vaccinated. Gradually, San Martín's army of the Andes took form. To his regular troops he added volunteers, refugees from Chile, and 1,500 slaves who served in exchange for their freedom.

Leads Surprise Attack Across Andes

On January 9, 1817, San Martín began one of the most spectacular operations in military history—the crossing of the Andes Mountains. With 9,000 mules, 1,600 horses, and 4,000 men, he crossed mountain passes as high as 12,500 feet above sea level. The cold and altitude, however, took its toll: many of his soldiers died, and only half the mules and a third of the horses survived. San Martín's troops arrived in Chacabuco, Chile on February 12, 1817, and soundly defeated the surprised Spanish army. He refused the governorship of Chile, preparing, instead, to meet any Spanish forces still in the region. Chile declared its independence on February 12, 1818, which San Martín then secured by defeating the remaining Spaniards at the bloody battle of Maipú in April.

The path for the invasion of Peru was now open. Because of turmoil in Argentina, however, San Martín did not receive the necessary funding for his army. His goal was delayed for two years. He finally received support from Chile and set sail for Lima (capital of Peru) in August 1820. He arrived with his army the following July to find the city deserted of Spanish forces. Even though he had never wanted political power, he became protector of Peru and proclaimed its independence. He could not secure this freedom, however, as he could not decisively defeat the Spanish forces that returned. As a result, many Peruvians thought he was simply holding onto power and called him a tyrant.

In 1822 San Martín traveled to Ecuador to meet with Simón Bolívar (see **Simón Bolívar**), who had fought for and won independence in the northwest regions of South America. No one is quite sure what occurred at this meeting, but an alliance between Bolívar and San Martín failed. He returned to Peru with nothing. In September he resigned as protector and gave his powers to the Peruvian Congress. Bitter over his treatment in South America, he left and spent the remainder of his life in Europe. While living in Boulogne-sur-Mer, France, San Martín died on August 17, 1850.

Sitting Bull

*Chief of the Hunkpapa branch
of the Teton Sioux*

Born c. 1830
Died December 15, 1890

At the famous battle of the Little Bighorn in Montana in 1876, the combined warriors of the Arapaho, the Cheyenne, and the Sioux massacred the Seventh Cavalry under the command of General George Armstrong Custer. This battle, often referred to as Custer's Last Stand, was also the last stand of the native tribes of the Great Plains. For years, the Sioux leader Sitting Bull had attempted to protect his people's hunting grounds and traditional way of life. He had brought Plains tribes together in hopes of finally repelling the white invaders. Even though the Native Americans won the battle at Little Bighorn, they could not win the war. The Americans continued to push westward, destroying the main source of survival the Sioux had—the buffalo. Stuck on a reservation, Sitting Bull lived out his final years trying to maintain his people's heritage and dignity.

Sitting Bull was born around 1830 in the present-day border area between the Dakotas and Montana. He was a member of the Hunkpapa, the most populous of the seven

"For years, the Sioux leader Sitting Bull had attempted to protect his people's hunting grounds and traditional way of life."

branches of the Teton (western) Sioux. The Sioux had originally lived in the woodlands of present-day Minnesota. In the seventeenth century, the Ojibwa, neighboring Sioux enemies, obtained guns from early European settlers and forced many Sioux to migrate southwestward. After the introduction of horses a century later, those Sioux adapted to life on the treeless plains.

The Sioux were not farmers but hunters, and buffalo (properly called the American bison) were extremely important to their way of life. Buffalo served as a source of food and other resources. The Sioux used every part of this animal, from the meat (for food) to the hides (for clothing and tents) to the bones (for tools). Buffalo also held a spiritual place in Sioux culture, and killing one was a rite of passage for young warriors. When Sitting Bull, whose childhood name was Slow, killed his first buffalo at the age of ten, his father gave him his adult name.

Sitting Bull's standing among the Hunkpapa warriors rose quickly. He joined his first war party when was 14. His fearlessness in battle earned him admission to the Strong Hearts, a warrior society, just a few years later. During a horse-stealing raid in 1856, a Crow chief shot him in the foot. Although Sitting Bull eventually developed a permanent limp, he gained honor that day by killing the chief. His reputation for bravery continued to grow as he risked his life in battles with rival tribes, including the Crow, the Flathead, and the Shoshone.

Discovery of Gold Brings Warfare

Sitting Bull did not face white soldiers until 1863. That year, the entire Sioux nation came under attack from the U.S. Army after Sioux tribes in Minnesota had killed 450 white settlers during an uprising. Over the next five years, warfare between the army and the Hunkpapa was almost constant. Gold discoveries in Montana increased the movement of whites through the northern plains. John Bozeman, a white guide, cut a trail for Montana-bound prospectors through the heart of Hunkpapa land. This Bozeman Trail only worsened the already poor relations between the tribes of the plains and the U.S. government.

After the army had suffered many losses, the government abandoned the Bozeman Trail and offered to sign a peace treaty in 1868. The Fort Laramie Treaty established a huge Sioux reservation in all of the Dakotas west of the Missouri River. Red Cloud, the most important Sioux chief at the time, accepted the treaty, but Sitting Bull did not. Although he and the Hunkpapa refused to live on the reservation, they were not bothered directly by the army. They continued their annual buffalo hunts.

This period of relative peace ended in 1874 when General Custer discovered gold while leading an expedition in the Black Hills of present-day South Dakota. Soon a rush of miners flooded this area of the reservation, violating the treaty. Sitting Bull, now a leader among the Teton Sioux, made an alliance with Crazy Horse (see **Crazy Horse**) of the Oglala Sioux and Two Moon of the Cheyenne. Over 3,000 warriors were brought together to protect their hunting grounds against the U.S. Army, which entered the area unprepared for the large enemy it was to face.

Massacre at Little Bighorn

Before heading into battle, Sitting Bull underwent the Sun Dance. In this ritual, a warrior's chest was pierced with rawhide thongs that were attached to a central pole. To tear himself free, a warrior would then dance until he was exhausted. Tired and in pain, Sun Dancers often would have visions. Sitting Bull foresaw victory. On June 25, 1876, he watched as the combined Sioux, Cheyenne, and Arapaho slaughtered General Custer and his Seventh Cavalry at the battle of Little Bighorn.

The U.S. Army could not completely defeat the Native Americans in battle, but it could defeat them by permitting white hunters in vast numbers to kill the buffalo. When the Plains buffalo were reduced almost to extinction, hunger soon led more and more Sioux chiefs to surrender. The government gave them food only after they agreed to a revised treaty that decreased the size of their reservation. Sitting Bull and his followers refused to surrender and escaped to Canada in May 1877. Unwilling to risk damaging its relationship with the U.S. government, the Canadian government declined to help Sitting Bull and his people. Buffalo soon became as scarce in Canada as they were in the Great Plains. In 1881, when they could no longer fight famine, Sitting Bull and his remaining followers crossed the border and surrendered.

Sitting Bull rejoined his fellow Sioux at the Standing Rock reservation in present-day North Dakota. Fighting to preserve Sioux culture, he refused to accept any American customs or conditions. In 1889 Sitting Bull and the Sioux began practicing the Ghost Dance religion, which had been developed among the Paiute in Nevada around 1870. This religion promised that white men would disappear from native lands and the nearly extinct buffalo would return to the plains. After dancing many hours, Ghost Dancers reportedly had visions of salvation. The government believed the ritual was a cover for a possible rebellion and sent soldiers to arrest Sitting Bull. When they arrived on December 15, 1890, a group of Ghost Dancers tried to prevent them from seizing the old chief. In the resulting fight, Sitting Bull was shot and killed.

John Smith

Leader of Jamestown settlement

Born c. 1580,
Willoughby, Lincolnshire, England

Died June 21, 1631,
London, England

John Smith was a soldier, an explorer, a geographer, and a writer. To this descriptive list some of Smith's colleagues might have added "rogue"—a villain or mischief-maker. It is true that Smith lived a life of adventure, but many people believe the stories he told about his adventures were just that—stories. Early in his career he was a mercenary—a soldier who fights for anyone for money. He learned how to survive, mainly on his own. In his late twenties, he sailed to the New World and helped found the Jamestown colony, the first permanent English settlement in America. Smith's strong character, which often put him at odds with others, made him an effective leader and rescued Jamestown from disaster.

Smith was born in Willoughby, Lincolnshire, England, to George and Alice Smith. He left school at the age of 15 to become a merchant's apprentice. After his father's death in 1596, he joined the French army and fought in the Netherlands. He returned to England in 1600, then went to fight Turkish invaders in Transylvania and Turkey. During these

> *"Smith's strong character, which often put him at odds with others, made him an effective leader and rescued Jamestown from disaster."*

battles he was captured and enslaved in Constantinople (present-day Istanbul, Turkey) where he met Elizabeth Rondee, an English woman also in captivity. After being sent north to present-day Bulgaria, Smith escaped to Russia. Before returning to England in 1605, Smith rescued Rondee from slavery.

At this time the Virginia Company of London was planning to establish a colony in present-day Virginia near Chesapeake Bay. Smith invested money in the company and at the end of 1606 set sail with the expedition, led by Captain Christopher Newport. Smith was one of seven councilors chosen to govern the colony, but during the voyage he was accused of trying to start a mutiny. When the settlers landed in Jamestown (named for King James I) in May of 1607, he was denied a seat on the council. He then spent his time exploring the area around the colony. Smith had the ability to learn languages quickly, and he soon traded for supplies with the surrounding Native American tribes. Many of them considered Smith the leader of the white settlement.

The council had elected Edward Wingfield governor of the colony, but he was weak. Smith directed the building of houses and of fortifications to protect the colony against attacks by native tribes, and the settlers soon saw him as their true leader. Few crops were planted that first summer, and many settlers died when a sickness swept through the colony in August. The council replaced Wingfield with John Ratcliffe, and Smith continued to help the colony by trading with the Native Americans.

Legend of Pochahontas

While exploring the area around Chesapeake Bay in December 1607, Smith and two companions were captured by the Powhatan tribe. Although the other men were killed, Smith survived. Legend states that Pochahontas, the 13-year-old daughter of Chief Powhatan, convinced her father to spare Smith's life. Whether or not this event happened, Pochahontas did visit the colony often afterward, bringing food and gifts. Smith returned to the starving colony in 1608 to find only 38 of the original 105 settlers alive. A few of his enemies accused him of the deaths of his companions, but he was saved from hanging by the arrival of Captain Newport and needed supplies from England.

Smith continued to explore Chesapeake Bay and its various rivers until he was selected governor of Jamestown in September 1608. He made the settlers strengthen the colony's defenses, build more houses, and plant more crops. Although they continued to struggle and often depended on trade with the Native Americans for food, the settlers survived under Smith's leadership.

The Virginia Company demanded that Smith and the settlers look for gold and build glass and tar factories. Smith refused, believing his job was to make the colony self-sufficient. When new supplies and settlers arrived from England in 1609, Smith received word from the company that he was being removed as governor. It is not known whether he intended to obey these orders, for shortly afterward he was badly burned in a gunpowder accident while exploring. Forced to seek treatment in England, he set sail in September, never to see Jamestown again.

Explores Coast of New England

Over the next few years, Smith recovered from his wound and wrote a book about his explorations around Jamestown, *A Map of Virginia* (published in 1612). With the help of a group of London merchants, he sailed back to America in 1614, exploring the area he named New England. He drew detailed maps of the coastline from present-day Nova Scotia to Rhode Island. Returning to England with a fortune in furs and fish, he proved the importance of establishing a permanent settlement in that region.

Smith set out in 1615 to found such a settlement, but a gale (strong wind) forced him back to port. He raised enough money to make another trip, only this time he was captured by French pirates. During his captivity, he wrote about his most recent explorations in *A Description of New England* (1616). He escaped from the pirates one night and weathered a storm in a rowboat. When he safely reached England, he learned the pirate ship had been sunk. Smith never returned to America after this. Through his writings, such as *The Generall Historie of Virginia, New England, and the Summer Isles* (1624), he continued to push for the settlement of English colonies in America. Smith died on June 21, 1631, in London, England.

Elizabeth Cady Stanton

Pioneering American feminist

*Born November 12, 1815,
Johnstown, New York*

*Died October 26, 1902,
New York, New York*

I n the years before the Civil War, American women did not exist according to the laws of many states. They could not inherit property, sign contracts, or bring a lawsuit to court. They did not have the right to vote, to hold public office, or to be tried in a court before a jury of their peers. Under the law, a woman was not protected from an abusive husband and any money she earned and any children she bore belonged to her husband. Because women were considered morally superior to men, one of the very few vocations open to them was motherhood. A few daring women, however, began calling for greater opportunities. In 1848, in Seneca Falls, New York, a group of these women gathered to draw attention to their plight and to work for change. This meeting launched the women's rights movement in the United States, and its leader was Elizabeth Cady Stanton.

Stanton was born in 1815 into an affluent family in Johnstown in upstate New York. Her parents, Daniel and Mary Livingston Cady, preferred boys, and one of Stanton's earliest

"Stanton sought to change not only the legal status of women but the way society viewed the very role of women."

memories was of her parents' disappointment on the birth of her younger sister. While growing up, Stanton tried to copy her brothers' academic achievements. She attended Johnstown Academy and studied Greek and mathematics. She also learned to ride and manage a horse and became a skilled debater. After she graduated in 1830, she convinced her father to allow her to attend the Troy Female Seminary in New York. It was one of the first women's academies to offer an advanced education equal to that of male academies. Here she studied logic, physiology, and natural rights philosophy.

Stanton's father was a judge and lawyer, and after she returned from the academy in 1833, she read law in his office and watched how he handled his cases. Seeing firsthand how women suffered legal discrimination, she resolved to change the laws. She also became involved at this time with the abolitionist (antislavery) movement and was exposed to progressive-thinking reformers. One of these was the journalist Henry Stanton, whom she married in 1840 against her father's wishes.

Discrimination Provokes Stanton to Act

Stanton traveled with her husband to London to attend the World Anti-Slavery Convention in June 1840. Here Stanton met Lucretia Mott, who was to become her close friend and intellectual mentor. When the convention refused to recognize women as legitimate delegates, Stanton and Mott were humiliated and angered. They resolved to call together a women's rights convention after they returned to America.

Eight years later, in Seneca Falls, New York, they carried through with their plan. On July 19, 1848, five women met to "discuss the social, civil, and religious condition and rights of women." Stanton, acting as leader, wrote the meeting's manifesto, the Seneca Falls Declaration of Sentiments. It included a women's bill of rights and listed demands for social equality, including women's suffrage (the right to vote). Public response to the declaration was highly critical, but soon other women met and began petitioning for suffrage. In 1851, Stanton met Susan B. Anthony (see **Susan B. Anthony**), whose organizing abilities complemented Stanton's more philosophical focus.

Their lifelong association did much for the advancement of women's rights.

The women's movement still remained within the larger antislavery movement, and when slavery came to an end, so did abolitionist support for women's rights. This betrayal led Stanton and Anthony in 1868 to create the independent National Woman Suffrage Association with Stanton as president. That same year, Stanton began publishing the *Revolution,* a women's rights newspaper. She refused to focus on suffrage alone, believing it was only a part of a greater program of social, economic, and political reform. Stanton sought to change not only the legal status of women but the way society viewed the very role of women. Her ideas were progressive. She protested the sexual abuse of women and championed the idea of husbands and wives equally caring for their children. She also lobbied to have men and women educated together.

Natural Rights

This political theory grew out of the ancient Greek philosophy of Stoicism and found its strongest voice during the Enlightenment, an eighteenth century philosophical movement. This theory holds that all members of society have certain basic rights, such as life, liberty, and the ownership of property. The English political philosopher and writer John Locke was perhaps the greatest supporter of this belief. He maintained that rational men understood and accepted these naturally existing rights. All individuals were entitled to them and no society had the right to take them away. The only function of a government was to protect those rights.

Documents the Fight for Women's Rights

In 1881 Stanton and Anthony published the first volume of the *History of Woman Suffrage,* a collection of writings about the movement's struggle. Two more volumes were published in the next five years. While many women's organizations had sprung up by this time, they differed in their opinions and approach. Many called only for moral reforms in society, not women's suffrage. To better achieve their goals, Stanton and Anthony united the two major women's groups into the National American Woman Suffrage Association in 1890.

Although Stanton was elected the first president, her radical stance on religion threatened to break the association apart. She believed organized religion promoted superstition and hostility to women. In 1895 she published *The Woman's*

Bible, a study of sexism in the Old Testament. A storm of protest arose and many of Stanton's colleagues condemned her. By the time she died in 1902, she was no longer the movement's leader. The Nineteenth Amendment, adopted by Congress in 1920, finally gave women the right to vote, but it did little to alter their lives. Change began only when Stanton's far-reaching ideas of equality were finally recognized in the last half of the twentieth century.

Tecumseh

Chief of the Shawnee
Born c. 1768
Died October 5, 1813

During the seventeenth century, the Shawnee were a divided people. Broken into two main groups, they moved throughout the western regions of the middle American colonies. By the mid-1700s they had reunited in their ancestral lands in the present-day state of Ohio. Yet they were soon again divided, this time by white settlers seeking land in the region known as the Old Northwest (made up of present-day states of Ohio, Illinois, Indiana, Wisconsin, and Michigan). Out of this split rose a young chief named Tecumseh, who was a fierce warrior and a strong leader. He struggled to bring together the Shawnee and all the tribes from the Great Lakes to the Gulf of Mexico to create a single Native American confederacy. In the end, his dream died along with him.

Tecumseh was the son of Methoataske and Puckeshinwa, a Shawnee chief. Throughout his childhood, he watched many fellow Shawnee perish in battles with white settlers over land. When he was six, he found his father dead from such a battle. The white invasion of Shawnee territory in Ohio was unstop-

"Tecumseh struggled to bring together the Shawnee and all tribes from the Great Lakes to the Gulf of Mexico to create a single Native American confederacy."

pable, and in 1779 over one-third of the tribe fled to present-day Missouri. Included in this group that left was Tecumseh's mother. He stayed behind and was raised by his sister Tecumpease, who taught him how to respect life, and his brother Cheesekau, who taught him how to hunt.

During the following years, Tecumseh trained to be a warrior. Because he showed great promise, he was given his name, which means "Shooting Star" or "Meteor." By the time he was 17, he displayed the qualities not only of a warrior but also of a leader. He criticized his tribesmen one day after a battle when they tortured a white settler to death with burning brands. Horrified, Tecumseh told them that such shameful acts dishonored a warrior. Deeply affected by Tecumseh's powerful stance, the Shawnee abandoned the practice of torturing prisoners. Now respected in his tribe, Tecumseh tried to rally the other Native American tribes of the Old Northwest (now called the Northwest Territory) against the whites.

Land Traded for Whiskey

Any chance of a confederation among these tribes was ruined in August 1794. The Unites States Army, led by General Anthony Wayne, crushed the combined Native American warriors at the battle of Fallen Timbers on Ohio's Maumee River. A year later, the chiefs of 12 different tribes signed the Greenville Treaty, surrendering most of Ohio, part of Indiana, and Detroit, Michigan, in exchange for money and kegs of whiskey.

Tecumseh, who had not attended the treaty signing, refused to honor it. He broke with other Shawnee leaders and became chief of his own village with about 100 rebel Shawnee warriors. In 1796 he married Mamate. She bore a son, Puchetha, but left soon after his birth. Some believe Tecumseh then met Rebecca Galloway, a white frontierswoman, who taught him to speak English, to read the Bible and Shakespeare, and to study world history. Whether this story is true, Tecumseh's concept of his people deepened at this time. He reasoned that Native American land belonged to all Native Americans. Therefore, no single tribe had the right to sign away land without the permission of all.

The whiskey traded to the Native Americans turned many of them into powerless alcoholics, and Tecumseh's brother Laulewasika was one of these. But in 1805, in a drunken trance, Laulewasika reportedly had a vision of the Great Spirit, the Shawnee master of life. When he awoke, he changed his name to Tenskwatawa ("the open door") and deemed himself the Shawnee Prophet. He preached to his people to reject all the ways of the white man and to return to Native American customs. Although Tecumseh accepted his brother's vision, some of the Shawnee doubted him. When the Prophet accurately predicted a solar eclipse, however, his holiness was no longer questioned.

Begins to Build Confederation

In 1808 the brothers founded a village known as Prophet's Town on the banks of the Tippecanoe River near present-day Lafayette, Indiana. Tecumseh then visited tribes from Missouri to Florida, preaching the need for a Native American confederacy. Within two years, one thousand warriors had gathered at Prophet's Town. The growing anger among these warriors soon alarmed General William Henry Harrison, governor of the Northwest Territory, and he called for peace talks in August 1810. Tecumseh tried to explain to Harrison his stand on the selling of Native American lands, but Harrison did not listen. The talks grew heated and soon broke down altogether.

Tecumseh believed war was inevitable, and in 1811 he set out to gather southern tribes to battle. While he was gone, the Shawnee Prophet thought he could destroy Harrison's militia, which was stationed near Prophet's Town. On November 7 he started what came to be known as the battle of Tippecanoe. Even though the fighting ended in a draw, most of the warriors fled after the battle. Tecumseh returned early the following year to find Prophet's Town and his hopes of Native American unity destroyed.

The Shawnee had fought for England during the American Revolution and did so again when the War of 1812 broke out between England and America. Tecumseh raised a band of warriors and helped the English major general Isaac Brock capture Detroit on August 16, 1812. This forever ended any American hopes of seizing lands in Canada. By the beginning of autumn, the Native Americans and the English controlled most of the Northwest Territory.

Their fortunes changed, however, when Brock was killed in October and replaced with the incompetent Colonel Henry Proctor. Under his command, battle losses for the combined English and Native American forces mounted. Tecumseh's army, which had numbered nearly 1,500 warriors by the spring of 1813, soon was reduced to about 500. On October 5 the combined forces met General Harrison and an American army of 3,500 men at the battle of the Thames, near present-day Chatham, Ontario. When the attack began, Proctor and the English retreated immediately. Tecumseh and his warriors, though badly outnumbered, bravely fought the losing battle. Any remaining hopes of a Native American confederation died along with Tecumseh that day.

Toussaint L'Ouverture

Ex-slave and Haitian revolutionary

Born in 1743,
Saint Domingue

Died April 7, 1803,
Fort de Joux, France

The present-day island of Hispaniola, the second largest in the Caribbean Sea, is divided between the Dominican Republic on the east and Haiti on the west. Over 500 years ago, this island was inhabited by the Arawak, a native people who had migrated from South America. They were eventually destroyed by the arrival of Europeans, led by Christopher Columbus in 1492. The Spanish soon controlled Hispaniola and established the colony of Santo Domingo on the eastern half of the island. They ignored the mountainous western half, allowing French pirates to build settlements there. In 1697 Spain signed the Treaty of Ryswick and surrendered the eastern half of the island to the French, who called it Saint Domingue.

The soil in Saint Domingue was fertile, and French colonists brought in slaves from Africa to work on vast coffee and sugar plantations. By the time the French Revolution began in 1789, almost 500,000 slaves worked strenuously in the heat of the Caribbean sun. As the Revolution's cry of "Lib-

"Although he failed to gain full independence for his people, Toussaint ended slavery on the island and came to symbolize the dream of liberty."

erty, Equality, Fraternity" grew, so did the slaves' own desire for freedom. In 1791 they revolted. Led by Toussaint L'Ouverture, this army of ex-slaves fought successfully against Spanish, English, and French forces. Although he failed to gain full independence for his people, Toussaint ended slavery on the island and came to symbolize the dream of liberty. In 1804, less than a year after his death, Hispaniola became the independent Haiti (Arawak for "land of mountains").

Toussaint was born in 1743 in Saint Domingue on a plantation near the present-day seaport of Cap-Haïtien. Because he was very intelligent, he did not work as a slave in the fields but served as a coach driver and waiter. Allowed use of the plantation library, he taught himself to read and to write. Shortly before 1791, he was freed from slavery. Toussaint now joined the ranks of the over 50,000 free blacks and mulattoes (those born of mixed races) who still had hardly any rights in the local society.

French Revolution Spurs Uprising

At the outbreak of the French Revolution, the mulattoes of Saint Domingue lobbied for representation in the National Assembly, France's new legislative body. Denied, they revolted in 1790 under the leadership of Vincent Ogé. One year later Ogé was defeated and executed. Out of this crisis rose a general slave revolt, led by Toussaint. When France and Spain went to war in 1793, he and his army joined the Spanish. He quickly won a series of victories over the French and became known as L'Ouverture (French for "the opening").

England invaded Hispaniola late in 1793 on the side of the Spanish. Fearing that England would restore slavery if it gained control of the island, Toussaint switched allegiance to France. In 1795 Spain gave rule of Santo Domingo to the French, but the English remained on Hispaniola. Because France was busy with battles overseas, Toussaint's army remained the principal fighting force against the English. His military operations, along with tropical diseases, quickly ravaged the European enemy. In 1798 England withdrew from the island.

This departure did little to end the fighting in Saint Domingue. Toussaint's main goal had always been to unify the island under the control of a free black population. This was threatened, however, by André Rigaud, a mulatto who had previously been allied with Toussaint. He declared a separate mulatto state in the southern province of Saint Domingue shortly after the English had left. Toussaint defeated Rigaud by 1800, but the campaign had been marked on both sides by massacre and inhumanity.

Gains Control of Entire Island

Since there was no effective French government in place on the island, Toussaint sought to realize his goal. Invading the eastern portion of Hispaniola, he destroyed any opposition. In January 1801 he conquered the capital of Santo Domingo and became master of the entire island. He wrote to the French leader Napoleon (see **Napoleon I Bonaparte**), claiming that the island had been united in the name of the French Republic. Both Toussaint and Napoleon knew this was not true.

Toussaint reorganized the government and declared himself governor general for life. He then selected a six-man convention to draft a new constitution. Even though it outlawed slavery on the island, the constitution dictated a strict system of labor. Everyone was forced to work on the plantations; those who did not work or who did poor work were often harshly punished. Toussaint explained to his people that these measures were necessary to improve Hispaniola and to keep it safe from outside threat. Indeed, living conditions did improve. Schools, bridges, and roads were built and foreign trade increased.

Napoleon, however, would not let this French colony slip out of his grasp. Early in 1802 he sent his brother-in-law General Charles Victor Emmanuel Leclerc and over 20,000 troops to reconquer the island. Awed by this army's size, many of Toussaint's military leaders quickly surrendered. With his remaining followers, Toussaint resisted the French for some months before he could only make simple raids in the island's interior. Leclerc was still unable to overtake him, and offered to sign a peace treaty if he surrendered. When Toussaint laid down his arms, however, Leclerc did not do the same. He had Toussaint arrested, placed in heavy chains, and sent to Fort de Joux, high in the French Alps. Unused to the cold climate, Toussaint died in a dungeon there on April 7, 1803. His followers carried on his goal, resuming their revolt. Less than a year later, they were free from French domination.

Sojourner Truth

American abolitionist and feminist

Born c. 1797,
Ulster County, New York

Died November 26, 1883,
Battle Creek, Michigan

A former slave who had been called Isabella, she chose the name Sojourner Truth because it represented the mission she believed God had given her. She explained in her autobiography, *Narrative of Sojourner Truth*, "I was to travel up and down the land, showing people their sins, and being a sign unto them." As a black woman, Truth was doubly discriminated against in a country founded on the idea of independent rights for all people. She never learned to read or to write, but became a moving speaker for black freedom and women's rights. While many of her fellow black abolitionists (people who campaigned for the end of slavery) spoke only to blacks, Truth spoke mainly to whites. While they spoke of violent uprisings, she spoke of reason and religious understanding.

She was born Isabella Baumfree around 1797 on an estate owned by Dutch settlers in Ulster County in southeast New York. She was the second youngest of the ten or twelve children of James Baumfree and his wife Elizabeth (known as "Mau-Mau Bett"). When her owner died in 1806, Isabella was

"As a black woman, she was doubly discriminated against in a country founded on the idea of independent rights for all people."

put up for auction. Over the next few years, she had several owners who treated her poorly. John Dumont purchased her when she was 13, and she worked for him for the next 17 years.

In 1817 the New York legislature passed a law granting freedom to slaves born before July 4, 1799. However, this law declared that those slaves could not be freed until July 4, 1827. While waiting ten years for her freedom, Isabella married a fellow slave named Thomas, with whom she had five children. As the date of her release came near, she realized that Dumont was plotting to keep her enslaved. In 1826 she walked away from his estate, leaving her husband and her children.

Wins Court Case to Regain Son

Three important events took place in Isabella's life over the next two years. She found refuge with Maria and Isaac Van Wagenen, who bought her from Dumont and gave her freedom. She then underwent a religious experience, claiming from that point on she could talk directly to God. Lastly, she sued to retrieve her son Peter, who had been sold illegally to a plantation owner in Alabama. In 1828, with the help of a lawyer, Isabella became the first black woman to take a white man to court and win.

Afterward, Isabella moved with Peter to New York City and began following Elijah Pierson, who claimed to be a prophet. He was soon joined by another religious fanatic known as Matthias, who claimed to be the Messiah. They formed a cult known as the "Kingdom" and moved to Sing Sing (renamed Ossining) in southeast New York in 1833. Isabella's faith in them soon shrank and she remained apart from their activities. When Matthias was arrested for murdering Pierson, however, she was accused of being an accomplice. A white couple in the cult, the Folgers, also claimed that Isabella had tried to poison them. For the second time, she went to court. After proven innocent in the Matthias case, she filed a slander suit against the Folgers. In 1835 she broke legal barriers again by becoming the first black person to win such a suit against a white person.

Isabella worked as a household servant in New York City for the next eight years. After a troublesome youth, Peter found work on a whaling ship and went off to sea. In 1843, deciding her mission was to preach the word of God, Isabella changed her name to Sojourner Truth and left the city. That summer she traveled throughout New England, calling her own prayer meetings and attending those of others. She supported herself with odd jobs and often slept out in the open air. At the end of the year, she joined the Northampton Association, a Massachusetts community founded on the ideas of freedom and equality. Here, Truth met social reformers and abolitionists, including Frederick Douglass (see **Frederick Douglass**), who introduced her to their movement.

During the 1850s, slavery became a heated issue in the United States. In 1850 Congress passed the Fugitive Slave Law, which allowed runaway slaves to be arrested and jailed without a jury trial. In 1857 the Supreme Court ruled in the Dred Scott Case that slaves had no rights as citizens and that the government could not outlaw slavery in new territories.

Lectures to Hostile Crowds

The times did not frighten Truth away from her mission. Her life story, written with the help of friend Olive Gilbert, was published in 1850. She then headed west and spoke about black freedom in town after town. Her unrehearsed lectures dealt with her own experiences as a slave. Her style, colorful and down-to-earth, softened the often hostile crowds she faced. While on her travels, Truth met many female abolitionists. She noticed that although women could be leaders in the movement, they could neither vote nor hold public office. Realizing she was discriminated against on two fronts, Truth became an outspoken supporter of women's rights.

By the mid-1850s, Truth had earned enough money from sales of her popular autobiography to buy land and a house in Battle Creek, Michigan. She continued her lectures, traveling to Ohio, Indiana, Iowa, Illinois, and Wisconsin. When the Civil War erupted in 1861, she visited black troops stationed near Detroit, Michigan, and offered encouragement. She met with U.S. President Abraham Lincoln (see **Abraham Lincoln**) in October of 1864. Afterward, she stayed in the Washington area, working in a hospital and counseling freed slaves in Virginia.

Following the end of the Civil War, Truth continued to work with freed slaves. After her arm had been dislocated by a streetcar conductor who had refused to let her ride, she fought for and won the right for blacks to share Washington streetcars with whites. For several years she led a campaign to have land in the West set aside for freed blacks, many of whom were poor and homeless after the war. She carried on her lectures for the rights of blacks and women throughout the 1870s. Failing health, however, soon forced Truth to return to her Battle Creek home. She died there on November 26, 1883.

Harriet Tubman

*American abolitionist, "conductor"
on the Underground Railroad*

*Born c. 1820,
Dorchester County, Maryland*

*Died March 10, 1913,
Auburn, New York*

For over 20 years before the Civil War, there existed in America a secret system for helping runaway slaves escape to freedom in the northern states or in Canada. Called the Underground Railroad, it was neither underground nor a railroad. It was only referred to as such because railroad terminology was used to describe the secret activities of the system. The slaves were called "passengers," those who aided them were "conductors," escape routes were "lines," and stopping places of safety were "stations."

Lines in the Underground Railroad went from Kentucky and Maryland to stations in New England and Canada. While most conductors were Quakers (whose religion forbids slavery) and abolitionists (northerners who fought against slavery), some conductors were free blacks or slaves who themselves had been passengers on the Railroad. One such escaped slave was Harriet Tubman. She singlehandedly led over 300 slaves to safety in the years 1850 to 1860.

"Tubman single-handedly led over 300 slaves to safety in the years 1850 to 1860."

Born around 1820 on a plantation in Maryland, Tubman was one of 11 children of Benjamin and Harriet Ross. Originally named Araminta, Tubman later adopted the first name of her mother. The young Tubman was often hired out to work for other families living near her owner. Unlike many slaves, she had the chance to return to her family between jobs. Like many slaves, however, she did not escape the brutalities of slavery: the permanent scars on her back testified to the many whippings she received while growing up.

Slave Uprising Spurs Desire to Escape

Slavery became even harsher after 1831. That year, a slave named Nat Turner led about 60 followers in a slave uprising in Virginia. Moving from plantation to plantation, he and his band killed 55 whites before they were eventually captured by the Virginia militia. Although terrified southern whites enacted stricter slave laws, the revolt had spread the ideas of rebellion and escape throughout the slave community. When Tubman was about 13, a fellow slave attempted to escape. The overseer (slave supervisor) tried to pursue the runaway, but Tubman blocked his path. Enraged, the overseer hurled a two-pound weight at the fleeing slave, only to strike Tubman in the forehead. The injury left her skull permanently pressed against her brain, and she experienced sudden unconscious spells for the rest of her life.

Although it was unusual for a slave and a free man to marry, Tubman met and married a free black named John Tubman in 1844. Unfortunately, Tubman's husband did not encourage her to escape and even threatened to betray her if she attempted to do so. Despite this threat, Tubman refused to give up her dream of freedom. In 1849 Tubman decided to escape alone. With the help of conductors along the Underground Railroad, she made her way north to Philadelphia, Pennsylvania.

Tubman supported herself by working as a cook and as a household servant. Within a year, she returned to Maryland to start freeing her relatives. She then began a decade-long campaign of conducting runaway slaves on the Underground Railroad. Known by the name of "Moses" (Hebrew prophet who led his people out of slavery in Egypt in 1400 B.C.), Tubman would appear in slave cabins on a Saturday night disguised as a man or as an old woman. She would then lead a group of passengers to safety the following morning, knowing slave owners would not pursue on a Sunday.

Leads "Passengers" to Safety in Canada

Soon after Tubman had begun her work on the Railroad, Congress enacted the Fugitive Slave Law of 1850. It required all runaway slaves to be returned to their owners without the benefit of a jury trial, and anyone caught helping a slave was heavily fined. Because she feared for the safety of her passengers in the United States, Tubman guided them to the small town of Saint Catherines in Ontario, Canada. Since slavery was outlawed in Canada, slaves were immediately free once they crossed the border. Saint Catherines also became her temporary home.

By 1857 Tubman had rescued her entire family. She then decided to risk settling in Auburn, New York, a strongly abolitionist community. There she met and worked with other reform-minded individuals like the poet and essayist Ralph Waldo Emerson and the women's rights movement leader Susan B. Anthony (see **Susan B. Anthony**). Perhaps the most famous of her associations was with the antislavery crusader John Brown. She helped him plan a raid on the federal arsenal at Harper's Ferry, Maryland, in November of 1859. Luckily, Tubman was too ill to take part in the unsuccessful raid in which Brown's sons were killed and he was captured.

During the Civil War, which began in April 1861, Tubman served as a nurse for sick and wounded Union soldiers in Florida and in South Carolina. She also acted as a spy, gathering information for a number of Union missions. On one occasion, she even organized and led a group of eight black men on a scouting assignment along the coast of South Carolina.

After the war, Tubman returned to Auburn to care for her parents and to continue to work for women's rights and other reform movements. Concerned about the poor condition of

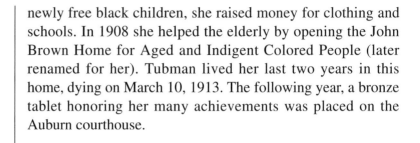

newly free black children, she raised money for clothing and schools. In 1908 she helped the elderly by opening the John Brown Home for Aged and Indigent Colored People (later renamed for her). Tubman lived her last two years in this home, dying on March 10, 1913. The following year, a bronze tablet honoring her many achievements was placed on the Auburn courthouse.

Booker T. Washington

Educator, founder of
Tuskegee Normal and Industrial Institute

Born in 1856,
Franklin County, Virginia

Died November 14, 1915,
Tuskegee, Alabama

Booker T. Washington began his life as a slave and ended it as one of the most respected African American educators in the United States. He founded the Tuskegee Normal and Industrial Institute (now the Tuskegee Institute), which became one of the country's most powerful institutions of higher learning for African Americans. Washington thought that hard work and thrift would lead to economic advancement. Only then could African Americans hope to achieve civil rights and social equality. Washington's emphasis on self-sufficiency helped thousands and led many others to recognize him as an African American leader. Because he refused to fight racism and injustice publicly, however, other African American intellectuals broke with him toward the end of his life.

Washington was born during the spring of 1856 on a plantation in Virginia. He was the son of a slave woman and an unknown white man. After the Civil War ended in 1865, he and his family, now free, moved to Malden, West Virginia. Because his family was poor, young Washington had to work

"Washington's emphasis on self-sufficiency helped thousands and led many others to recognize him as an African American leader."

with his stepfather (whose last name he adopted) in the local salt furnaces and coal mines. At first, he could only attend school at night. Later, his stepfather allowed him to go during the day as long as he worked both before and after school.

Washington's deep desire for an education led him in 1872 to travel 500 miles to the Hampton Institute in Virginia, one of the first coeducational schools for African Americans. Founded in 1868 by Samuel Chapman Armstrong, Hampton emphasized an education based on practical skills. During his three years there, Washington worked as a janitor to help pay for his school and living expenses. He graduated with honors in 1875 and returned to Malden to teach school for African American children. In 1878 he studied for eight months at the Wayland Seminary in Washington, D.C. Afterward, he became an instructor at Hampton, teaching a new program for Native Americans.

Builds Tuskegee Normal and Industrial Institute

In 1881 Washington received his greatest opportunity: Armstrong chose him to become principal of a new school for African Americans in Tuskegee, Alabama. When he arrived on the site of the campus, however, he found only an abandoned plantation—the school had yet to be built. Over the next few years, Washington supervised the planting of crops and the making of bricks. By 1888 the buildings of the Tuskegee Normal and Industrial Institute were spread out over 550 acres. Over 400 students were enrolled in such trade programs as farming, carpentry, printing, shoemaking, tinsmithing, and cooking.

From its beginning, Tuskegee fully reflected Washington's own philosophy of self-help, self-respect, and practical learning. To build character, students underwent strict discipline, which often consisted of daily inspections and military drills. In addition to studies, cleanliness and thrift were priorities at the school. Many members of Tuskegee's faculty objected to the school's emphasis on manual education programs. Washington, however, believed they were necessary in order for African Americans to achieve economic independence.

Washington preached his philosophy outside of Tuskegee through speeches before several local and state organizations. His reputation as a public speaker grew. In 1895 he was asked to address the Cotton States and International Exposition in Atlanta, Georgia. Here, he gave a controversial speech stating that African Americans should concentrate on economic equality rather than social equality. Many white Americans applauded his views and hailed him as the leader of his race. Washington's autobiography, *Up From Slavery* (published in 1901), also added to his reputation in white society. In the book, he explained how he overcame his poor childhood through hard work and thrift. Impressed by Washington's self-help philosophy, many wealthy white northerners made generous financial donations to Tuskegee.

Washington's influence soon spread beyond Tuskegee. In 1892 he organized the first Tuskegee Negro Conference. Thousands of rural African Americans were exposed to new agricultural techniques at these annual conferences. In 1900 he established the National Negro Business League, which he hoped would promote ways for African Americans to become economically independent. Through his ties to wealthy white businessmen, such as Andrew Carnegie and George Eastman, Washington helped raise money for many other African American causes and institutions.

Secretly Fights Racism

Because of these ties, however, Washington could not speak out about the growing racism in America. Beginning in the 1880s, Southern states began enacting Jim Crow laws, which segregated blacks and whites in everything from restaurants to railroad cars. In 1896 the U.S. Supreme Court ruled in *Plessy v. Ferguson* that "separate but equal" facilities for blacks and whites were constitutional. Washington pleaded with legislators to change these laws, but when they refused, he did not push them any further. In private, however, he urged other African Americans to lead protests. He also contributed money anonymously to have these laws challenged in courts.

With an increase in racist laws and hate crimes, however, African American leaders remained quiet no longer. Many of them, including W. E. B. Du Bois (see **W. E. B. Du Bois**), openly criticized Washington for his lack of action. After 1905, African Americans were split into two rival groups with different visions of racial progress. When he died on November 14, 1915, Washington was no longer considered a leader on social issues. But Tuskegee, having grown to over 1,500 students at the time of his death, ensured that Washington would be remembered.

George Washington

First president of the United States

Born February 22, 1732,
Westmoreland County, Virginia

Died December 14, 1799,
Mount Vernon, Virginia

Few people in history have been given the chance to hold such unlimited power as George Washington. After the American Revolution ended, he could have used his success to become king of America. No one at that time would have been surprised or would have even minded. But Washington was devoted to the ideals of democracy and would not turn America into a copy of the country he had just fought during the Revolution. There is a story about a discussion between English king George III and Benjamin West, the American historical painter appointed to work for him. When the king asked West what he thought Washington would do after the war, West replied that Washington would go home to his farm. "If he does," said George III, "he will be the greatest man in the world." Washington did just that, and many people at the time agreed with the English king's belief.

Washington was born in 1732 on a farm on the banks of Pope's Creek in eastern Virginia. His father, Augustine Washington, owned several farms and four dozen slaves. When he

"Washington was devoted to the ideals of democracy and would not turn America into a copy of the country he had just fought during the Revolution."

died in 1743, young George inherited a farm near Fredericksburg and ten slaves. Though he studied reading, writing, and math, Washington received very little formal education. He dreamed of adventure and wanted to become an English naval officer, but his domineering mother, Mary Ball Washington, forbade it. Having some talent in arithmetic, he then took up surveying, and at the young age of 17 became the surveyor of Culpeper County. The intimate knowledge he gained of frontier lands would come to serve him well during his military years.

Washington's half-brother Lawrence, a favorite of his, owned Mount Vernon and was an officer in the county militia. When Lawrence died in 1752, Washington inherited not only Mount Vernon but Lawrence's military post as well. He would soon begin his spectacular military ascent. By 1753 France and England were heading into what became known as the French and Indian War over land claims in the Ohio Valley. The governor of Virginia sent Washington on a dangerous mission to tell the French to vacate a fort on English-controlled territory in Pennsylvania. The French refused to obey, forcing Washington to return with word of their plans. On his way back, he barely escaped death from icy weather conditions and Native American attacks.

Made a lieutenant colonel, Washington then led 400 men to build Fort Necessity near French-controlled Fort Duquesne on the site of present-day Pittsburgh. The ensuing battles marked the beginning of the war on American soil. Even though he lost Fort Necessity to the French, Washington went on to distinguish himself in combat. Named commander in chief of the Virginia militia in 1755, he spent the following few years protecting Virginia settlers from attacks by Native Americans allied with the French. Unwilling to make a career out of the military, Washington resigned his post in 1759 and married a wealthy widow, Martha Dandridge Custis. Over the next 15 years, he served as a member of the Virginia House of Burgesses (the lower house of the colonial legislature) and supervised his plantation at Mount Vernon.

Drawn to Fight for Independence

Washington's peaceful life was soon shattered by the call for American independence. The religious and political views of the colonial Americans and the English began to differ greatly by the 1750s. And when the English government tightened its control over the colonies in the 1760s, Americans began to revolt. In 1765 England passed the Stamp Act, which required the colonists for the first time to pay a tax on newspapers, land deeds, and other legal documents. The colonists refused to be taxed by a government they did not elect, and the famous colonial cry of "No taxation without representation" arose. England repealed this tax only to pass others, and disputes over these taxes and English rule erupted into the American Revolution on April 19, 1775. Two months later, the Second Continental Congress unanimously selected Washington to lead a force against the English.

As commander, Washington's main task was to create an army and maintain it. This army, composed mostly of inexperienced soldiers from state militias who served for only a few months at a time, had to be constantly retrained. The short supplies of food, clothing, equipment, and munitions added to the problem. After a few initial victories, Washington and the Continental army suffered losses and had to retreat. The army's morale was at its lowest in the late autumn of 1776, but this changed with Washington's decision to attack when least expected. On Christmas night the Continental army crossed the ice-filled Delaware River, marched eight miles to Trenton, New Jersey, and surprised the English who were sleeping off the previous day's celebrations. A week later, it captured another English force at the nearby city of Princeton.

The positive effect of these victories, however, was short-lived. Supplies were still badly needed, and the harsh winter of 1777 to 1778 nearly destroyed the Continental army. Camped at Valley Forge, Pennsylvania, Washington's men suffered—over 2,500 of them died from starvation and the cold. Only his support and leadership led the remaining troops through this difficult period. In the spring, France joined the American cause and the war tide turned. One and one-half years later, on October 19, 1781, English general Charles Cornwallis surrendered to Washington after the battle of Yorktown in southeast Virginia.

Accepts the Presidency

In 1783 England signed the Treaty of Paris granting the colonies independence. Washington, viewed as the most important man in America, shocked everyone when he resigned from the army and retired to Mount Vernon. But the new government needed a stronger set of rules than the Articles of Confederation (approved in 1781), and he agreed to preside over the Constitutional Convention called in 1787. The new Constitution of the United States created the presidency, and Washington was the unanimous first choice for the office. Although reluctant to leave his private life, he accepted.

Washington spent his first term creating tax laws and establishing federal departments, such as the court system. He wanted the presidency to remain nonpartisan (neutral to political sides), and he appointed men of differing views to cabinet positions. But his idea of a nonpartisan government soon faded when two political parties—the Federalists and the Democratic Republicans—formed over the debate of states' rights. The Federalists, led by Secretary of the Treasury Alexander Hamilton, believed in a strong central government. The Democratic Republicans (ancestors of the modern Democratic party), led by Secretary of State Thomas Jefferson (see **Thomas Jefferson**), believed the government should handle only foreign affairs.

Quarrels between the two sides grew bitter, with Washington in the middle. Believing the government needed to control both foreign and domestic matters, Washington sided with Hamilton. Jefferson then resigned from the cabinet. The Whiskey Rebellion in 1794 tested Washington's belief in a strong government. Frontier farmers in western Pennsylvania resisted a tax placed on whiskey. Washington sent in federal troops and the rebellion was put down without bloodshed. More important, Washington had shown that the government had the strength and means to enforce federal laws.

Foreign affairs were equally troublesome. France declared war on England in 1793 and wanted America's help. Washington felt the country could not afford to become involved overseas, and he kept America neutral. For this stance, he was highly criticized. Weary of constant bickering, Washington insisted on retiring when his second term ended in 1797. He returned to Mount Vernon, spending his remaining time managing his plantation and receiving numerous visitors. He died suddenly on December 14, 1799, two days after inspecting his estate during a cold rainstorm. The news saddened the world, and tributes to Washington were paid throughout. Perhaps the most significant was a grand salute fired off by the guns of the English navy.

Roger Williams

Founder of Rhode Island

Born c. 1603,
London, England

Died 1683,
Providence, Rhode Island

"Williams founded Rhode Island on an idea that grew to become a basic part of the American tradition—the separation of church and state."

In Geneva, Switzerland, there is a memorial to the Protestant Reformation, the religious revolution that began in Germany in the sixteenth century and spread across Western Europe. There are statues of the German Martin Luther (see **Martin Luther**), the Frenchman John Calvin, and the Swiss Ulrich Zwingli. Among these statues of the leaders of the fight for religious freedom stands one honoring a single American—Roger Williams. When he found no place in the American colonies that supported his belief in the right of people to worship freely, he built a place in the wilderness that did. Williams founded Rhode Island on an idea that grew to become a basic part of the American tradition—the separation of church and state.

Williams was born around 1603 into a comfortable household in London, England. His father, James Williams, was a moderately successful merchant tailor and his mother, Alice Pemberton, was a descendent of a minor noble family. The young Williams received an excellent education. His abilities in Latin and shorthand caught the attention of the famous English lawyer Sir Edward Coke, who hired Williams to work as his secretary and assistant for five years. Coke then paid for William's education at Pembroke College, Cambridge, from 1623 through 1627.

While at Cambridge, Williams accepted the religious beliefs of the Puritans, members of the Church of England who objected to the use of Roman Catholic customs in worship services. Believing Church rulers were corrupt, they also wanted to reform and "purify" the way the Church was run (hence their name, Puritans). After graduating, Williams became a chaplain in the wealthy Puritan household of Sir William Mashem. Later that same year he married Mary Bernard, a maid in a neighboring household.

Williams soon identified more with the Separatists, a group of Puritans who wanted to break away from the Church of England. Since King Charles I persecuted Separatists, many of them left England for America. In December 1630, Williams and his wife joined this migration. When they arrived in Boston early in 1631, Williams was offered the pastorship of the local church. He immediately refused it, though, believing most members of the church did not share his strong Separatist beliefs. He quickly alarmed Boston leaders by insisting that the government should have no say in church matters and that the churches of Massachusetts should reject the Church of England as un-Christian.

Banished for His Beliefs

Williams accepted a position with a church in Salem, but authorities in Boston pressured the church to withdraw its offer. Williams was forced out. He then traveled to Plymouth Colony (see **William Bradford**) and served as an assistant pastor for two years. In 1633 the Salem church asked him to return to assist its ailing pastor. When the pastor died the following year, Williams took control. His views did not soften. Instead, he increased his call for the separation of church and state. The General Court of Massachusetts then tried and convicted him of the crime of "teaching dangerous opinions." In

October 1635 Williams was banished from the Massachusetts Bay Colony, and he fled south into the wilderness of present-day Rhode Island.

Since the day he had arrived in America, Williams had been concerned with the unfair treatment of Native Americans by settlers. He survived the winter of 1636 with the help of the Narragansett, one of the nearby native tribes, and purchased land from them on which he built a settlement. In addition to farming, Williams spent his time studying the Narragansett language and wrote *A Key Into the Language of America*. It was the first serious study of a Native American culture and language written in English.

Williams named his settlement Providence and it became a home for all religious refugees. So diverse were the early settlers of this area that it was known as "the place where men think otherwise." Williams founded Providence on the idea of the separation of church and state. But beyond this, he defended the right for people to worship as they pleased, and forced no one to attend any specific church. All groups who were shunned in other colonies were welcomed to settle and to practice their beliefs in Providence.

Becomes Leader of Rhode Island

By 1643 four settlements existed in the Narragansett Bay area of Rhode Island, and Williams felt he needed to protect their borders against other colonies. He traveled to England to secure a colonial charter that set the boundaries of Rhode Island and placed the settlements under one government. While there, he published his most famous work, *The Bloudy Tenent of Persecution for the Cause of Conscience,* in which he defended the right to practice any religion freely without government interference. When Williams returned to Providence in 1654, he was elected president of Rhode Island and served until 1657.

In 1675 the Wampanoag, Narragansett, and Nipmuck tribes joined forces against the English settlers in King Philip's War. Murders, broken treaties, and other abuses against the native tribes by the governments of the Puritan colonies led to this war. King Philip was the English name given to Meta-comet, chief of the Wampanoag. Williams had tried desperately to prevent the war, but when Native American braves killed a number of settlers during a raid, the battle was on. Even though he was over 70 years old, Williams served as a captain in the Providence militia. He helped negotiate a peace treaty the following year, but by then the Native Americans were virtually wiped out from southern New England. Williams spent the remainder of his life in Providence, dying there in 1683 at the age of 80.

Emiliano Zapata

Rebel general during the Mexican Revolution

Born August 8, 1879,
Anenecuilco, Morelos, Mexico

Died April 10, 1919,
Morelos, Mexico

"Under the battle cry of 'land and freedom,' Emiliano Zapata fought and died in the struggle to restore the land rights of his people."

Porfirio Díaz took control of Mexico in the late nineteenth century. He helped modernize the country and improved its economy. Under his leadership, however, Mexico's social conditions worsened. He favored only those people who supported his policies, especially the owners of the haciendas—huge estates or plantations. The *campesinos* (native peasants) sank deeper into poverty. They were denied any voice in the government, and any land they owned was seized by the government. When Mexicans finally revolted against the government in 1910, starting the Mexican Revolution, one man rose to champion the cause of the *campesinos*. Under the battle cry of "land and freedom," Emiliano Zapata fought and died in the struggle to restore the land rights of his people.

Zapata was born in 1879 in the village of Anenecuilco in the Mexican state of Morelos. Growing up among the ever-expanding sugar plantations, he only briefly attended elementary school. He and his family were not peones—poor workers who slaved away on the haciendas. They owned a small tract of land and some livestock, and he learned to be a mule and horse trainer. Despite being slightly better off economically, Zapata and his family shared many of the problems of the *campesinos*. This included having portions of their land unexpectedly seized by hacendados (owners of haciendas) and others in power.

In 1909, just before the Revolution began, the people of Anenecuilco voted Zapata president of the village council. His main job was to try to protect the land holdings of his fellow villagers. When Francisco Madero, son of a wealthy rancher from northern Mexico, called for a rebellion to overthrow the Díaz government in November 1910, Zapata did not initially join in. Only after Madero promised that land would be returned to the *campesinos* if the uprising were successful did Zapata help raise an army.

Zapatistas Continue the Fight for Land

By May 1911, scattered rebel victories had forced Díaz to resign his position and to flee to Europe. In the new elections held in October, Madero won the presidency. He demanded that Zapata and his followers, called Zapatistas, lay down their arms. They refused to do so until the new president met their demands for land reform. Madero, however, had no intention of breaking up the haciendas and distributing the land among the *campesinos*. Because the Zapatistas continued their revolt, Madero called them bandits.

On November 25, 1911, Zapata issued his own revolutionary platform, the *Plan de Ayala*. He demanded that all illegally seized land be returned to its rightful owners and that one-third of the land of all haciendas be given to the *campesinos*. To prove he wasn't just a bandit, Zapata set up commissions to distribute any returned land fairly. He also organized banks to help the *campesinos* buy land.

When the Madero government refused to recognize his plan, Zapata and his followers began a series of ambushes. Since they lacked food, clothing, weapons, and ammunition, the Zapatistas looted supplies from enemy haciendas and towns they captured. In February 1913, Madero's top general,

Victoriano Huerta, seized control of the government and assassinated Madero. Huerta proved to be a dictator, however, and forces loyal to Madero drove him from office in August 1914. The politician Venustiano Carranza then assumed the presidency.

Zapata submitted his *Plan de Ayala* to the new president, but Carranza had no intention of meeting his demands. Zapata then met fellow revolutionary Pancho Villa in Xochimilco on the outskirts of Mexico City on December 4, 1914. The two men agreed to continue the Revolution against Carranza. The alliance with Villa and his Army of the North, however, was of little help to the Zapatistas. Villa promised to send supplies to Zapata and his men, but never did. Between April and June of 1915, Villa's army suffered crushing defeats, allowing the federal army to concentrate on the Zapatistas.

Revolution Turns Bloody

Although the Zapatistas had shrunk from 20,000 to 5,000 by the end of 1916, they remained a serious threat. Federal troops marched into Morelos and began a brutal campaign to recapture villages and towns. The almost constant fighting was perhaps the worst of the Revolution. Villagers were taken hostage or forced to resettle in other regions. Entire towns were burned to the ground. Captured Zapatistas were murdered as were those people suspected of helping them. In response, Zapata and his men attacked targets around Mexico City. On one occasion, they blew up a train with 400 passengers aboard. Many of those killed were civilians.

While Carranza remained firmly in power, the Zapatistas began to split apart. Many were hungry and tired of the fighting. They wanted to negotiate a peace settlement even if it meant the *Plan de Ayala* would not be accepted. Zapata disagreed, refusing to compromise on his mission. Only after he achieved land reform would he return to the quiet life of his farm and horses. Although Zapata had regained control of Morelos by 1917, he could not celebrate. While the *campesinos* of Morelos strongly supported his cause, other Mexicans, especially northern rebels, did not. This lack of national support would ultimately prevent his triumph in the Revolution.

An act of treachery brought about Zapata's end in 1919. Jesús Guajardo, a colonel in the federal army, wrote to Zapata saying he and 500 of his men wanted to join the Zapatistas. Zapata was suspicious and asked Guajardo to execute several former Zapatistas who had defected to the federal side. Guajardo agreed and did so. A meeting between the two men was then set up for April 12, 1919, at the Hacienda de Chinameca. When Zapata rode into the walled estate, a bugle sounded an honor call. The soldiers lining the entrance then fired two rounds into the unsuspecting revolutionary leader. Other rebels carried on the cause, but the goals of Zapata and the *campesinos* were never fully met.

Picture Credits

Photographs and illustrations appearing in *World Leaders: People Who Shaped the World* were received from the following sources:

Courtesy of Chester Beatty Library, Dublin: volume 1: p. 4; **courtesy of Chinese Information Service:** volume 1: p. 14; **AP/Wide World Photos:** volume 1: pp. 37, 99; **courtesy of the USSR State Archival Fund:** volume 2: p. 256; **courtesy of Caisse Nationale des Monuments Historiques et des Sites, Paris:** volume 2: p. 260; **courtesy of the Organization of American States:** timeline; volume 3: pp. 342, 471, 496; **courtesy of the John F. Kennedy Library,** photo no. AR6283A: timeline; volume 3: p. 391; **courtesy of Franklin D. Roosevelt Library:** volume 3: pp. 442, 447.

Master Index

Boldface indicates profiles